If you have breath in your lungs, you're probably busy. (And maybe even out of breath!) It's easy to get caught up in tasks and to-dos, but in the midst of the manic we lose the beauty of life in exchange for busyness. Stop running in circles and start living in the moments.

With humor and humility, Alli not only shares her candid failures and follies but gives practical and useful tips on how to break patterns of busyness. Her experiences allow us to enter into her story and learn how to get off the hamster wheel and start living the life we always wanted to live! It's time to *Break Busy*.

BIANCA JUAREZ OLTHOFF, teacher, speaker, and author of *Play with Fire: Discovering a Fierce Faith, Unquenchable Passion, and a Life-Giving God*

I don't know when or how busyness became a status symbol, but I am so glad that in *Breaking Busy*, Alli Worthington is calling us all back to a better way of living!

JON ACUFF, *New York Times* bestselling author of *Do Over: Rescue Monday, Reinvent Your Work, and Never Get Stuck*

Breaking Busy speaks into the life of every woman who strives to spend her time, energy, and talents on the most important priorities in her life. As a working-mother authority, Alli Worthington transparently guides her readers through her own life transitions and tough choices, sharing her insights in both a thoughtful and whimsical way. This book brilliantly combines storytelling with action planning for life-impacting change. *Breaking Busy* is a must-read for every busy woman searching for peace and purpose amidst the demands of a crazy life!

DEE ANN TURNER, Vice President, Corporate Talent, Chick-fil-A, Inc.; author of *It's My Pleasure: The Impact of Extraordinary Talent and a Compelling Culture*

Alli Worthington has learned the difference between simply having *a full life* and truly experiencing *life to the full*. She shares her secrets in this warm, funny, and wise book that will help all of us finally trade "busy" for God's very best.

HOLLEY GERTH, *Wall Street Journal* bestselling author of *You're Already Amazing*

Breaking Busy is a great read for women who feel like they don't have quite enough hours in the day to finish their to-do list — in other words, most of us! Alli's voice is authentic and witty, plus her content is uber-practical. Whether you're a harried mom with french fries littering the floor boards of your minivan or a high-level executive with more meetings than your iCal can keep up with, this book will help you navigate the next season of your life with significantly less stress and a lot more genuinely relaxed smiles.

LISA HARPER, Bible teacher, adoptive mom, and author of *Believing Jesus: Are You Willing to Risk Everything*

Alli Worthington strikes you as the kind of girl who can have and do it all. She's remarkably successful, juggles a wild and crazy family, and yet manages to always show up looking smart and snappy. If I didn't know her better I would be intimidated! But here is the truth: Alli is one of the most genuine, thoughtful, strong, and stable women I know. Her book *Breaking Busy* is an honest, insightful, and hilarious telling of her own journey to (as the subtitle says) "find peace and purpose in a world of crazy." Read it and know you're not alone and that you too can break busy.

JENNI CATRON, leadership coach and author of *The 4 Dimensions of Extraordinary Leadership*

No offense to anyone else, but I think Alli Worthington might have written this book just for me. I needed *Breaking Busy!* — but I'm not alone. This book is practical, yes, but it's also wise and warm, like a good friend who helps us all to find the real way forward into a life less busy and more fulfilling.

SARAH BESSEY, author of *Out of Sorts: Making Peace with an Evolving Faith*

The secret to a life of fulfillment is all about getting off the busy train. In *Breaking Busy*, Alli Worthington will show you just how to ban busy, live better, and laugh all the way home.

CLAIRE DIAZ-ORTIZ, author and Silicon Valley innovator

Alli Worthington's *Breaking Busy* is a breath of fresh air. Her honest storytelling and practical advice will resonate with any person who has uttered the words "I'm so busy!"

JESSICA N. TURNER, author of *The Fringe Hours: Making Time for You*

BREAKING
BUSY

BREAKING BUSY

HOW TO FIND PEACE & PURPOSE
IN A WORLD OF CRAZY

ALLI WORTHINGTON

ZONDERVAN

Breaking Busy
Copyright © 2016 by Alli Worthington

Requests for information should be addressed to:
Zondervan, 3900 *Sparks Dr. SE, Grand Rapids, Michigan 49546*

Library of Congress Cataloging-in-Publication Data

Worthington, Alli.
        Breaking busy : how to find peace and purpose in a world of crazy /
    Alli Worthington.
            pages   cm
        ISBN 978-0-310-34222-9 (pbk.) — ISBN 978-0-310-34224-3 (ebook) —
    ISBN 978-0-310-06705-4 (mobile app)
        1. Christian life. 2. Christian women—Religious life. I. Title.
    BV4501.3.W68   2016
    248.4—dc23   2015026533

Published in association with literary agent Jenni Burke of D.C. Jacobson & Associates
LLC, an Author Management Company www.dcjacobson.com

Cover design: *Lori Danelle Wilson*
Cover photos: *Shutterstock®*
Interior design: *Kait Lamphere*

First printing December 2015 / Printed in the United States of America

To my husband, Mark —

Thank you for your love, your patience,
your leadership, and your courage.
You are my rock when I get shaky.
You are my steady when I freak out.
Thank you for choosing me all those years ago.
I cherish this journey with you —
every up, every down, every crazy turn.
I can't imagine taking this ride
with anyone else by my side.

CONTENTS

Foreword by Christine Caine. 13

1. CAPACITY
Finding Your Sweet Spot in a World of Crazy Busy. . 17

2. RELATIONSHIPS
*Finding Your Connection in a World
of Acquaintances* 41

3. CALLING
Finding Your Purpose in a World of Striving 59

4. EDITING
Finding God's Best in a World of Options 79

5. THOUGHTS
Finding Your Peace in a World of Worry. 101

6. TRADITIONS
Finding Your Groove in a World of Expectations . . . 119

7. TIME
Finding Your Rhythm in a World of Overwhelm . . . 139

8. DECISIONS
Finding Your Confidence in a World of Choices 155

9. COMMUNICATION
Finding Your Voice in a World of Noise 173

10. WORTH

Finding Your Value in a World of Never Good Enough........................195

Epilogue..207
Acknowledgments...........................211

FOREWORD

by Christine Caine

Busy is intoxicating. We live in a day and age when we seem to get high on being *busy*. In fact we wear the label like a badge of honor, a secret seal of approval, a validation and proof of our worthiness. If we're not *busy*, constantly racing from one thing to the next, then we obviously must not be doing enough ... right? On the surface we seem to love the rush of having more things to do than time to do them in, but deep down we have a nagging sense that there must be more to our short time on earth than not having enough time to live the abundant life Jesus said he came to give us. Who has time for abundant living when we are clearly not even barely living?

But maybe it's the *busy* that's making us crazy. And maybe some of us are so *busy* being *busy* that we're missing out on God's purpose and plan for our lives.

In the following pages, my friend Alli Worthington will give you a new perspective on this concept she calls *breaking busy*. She will make you laugh out loud, perhaps shed a tear, and challenge you to think long and hard about the impact *busyness* has on your everyday life — the choices you make, your interactions with the people closest to you, and your relationship with God. Alli is honest, straightforward, prophetic, and the real deal. Her full disclosure, sweet vulnerability, and funny storytelling will make you realize that you're not alone in this struggle with *busyness*. The woman has a husband, five sons, and a demanding fulltime job. Let's just go ahead and assume she might just have some wisdom to speak into all our lives about breaking busy.

My prayer is that as you read this book you will learn to let go of busy and take up your purpose. Doing the right thing is far more energizing than simply doing anything and everything. We only have one life and this life is too important to waste by being busy. If you apply the principles Alli outlines in the book, you will not only feel less stressed and more fulfilled, but you will also live a life of fruitfulness.

Trust me, fruitful is way more effective than busy.

Love, Chris

ONE

CAPACITY

*Finding Your Sweet Spot in
a World of Crazy Busy*

I'm very attached to my iPhone. Attached enough that when I can't find it, my whole life stops until it's found.

Years ago, I was on a business trip to San Jose, California, and due to horrible planning and judgment on my part, I scheduled my return flight to Nashville at 6:00 a.m. I knew better than to get a flight at 6:00 a.m. I had burned myself before, getting too little sleep and doing too much, but like a defiant toddler who insists that last doughnut won't give her a stomachache *this time*, I insisted I needed that early flight so I could fit more in my day. What I forgot was that a 6:00 a.m. flight meant I had a 2:00 a.m. wake-up call. Wake-up calls that early in the morning mean one of three things: you hate yourself; the person who booked your flight hates you; or you are too prideful to know your own limits.

With bleary eyes, I flopped on the shuttle a little after 3:00 a.m. and stretched out across a whole row of seats, hoping to sleep just a little longer on the forty-five-minute trip to the San Francisco airport. Any other time, I would have stayed awake on the drive across the Bay Bridge and watched the fog roll around the hills coming off the bay. Growing up in the foothills of Tennessee, I never imagined I would be able to travel to cities I read about in magazines, and the magic of beautiful San Francisco wasn't lost on me. But at 3:00 a.m., you can't see the gorgeous fog rolling around the hills anyway, and all I cared about was getting a few more minutes of sleep.

A little before 4:00 a.m., the shuttle driver bellowed, "San Francisco International." For a second, I wasn't quite sure where I was or even who I was. Those four hours of sleep from the night before obviously were not enough for me. Realizing I had drooled on the seat (don't judge me), I wiped the corners of my mouth, grabbed my purse (which always weighs 147 pounds when I travel), pulled my suitcase off the rack, and shuffled into the airport.

Wincing at the bright airport light, I made my way to the long line to check in. I propped my suitcase against my leg, looked into my purse for my phone, and found … nothing.

You know how your stomach falls just a bit when you think you can't find your phone and then there's that moment of relief that comes when you find it inside a pocket or in between too many papers in your bag? Yeah, me too. I love that feeling.

That moment never came. I knew instantly I had left my phone in the shuttle, and the weight of that realization left me in a panic. How in the world had I left my phone? It must have just blended in to the seat in the dark shuttle. I felt sick, physically sick. I think the only thing that could have made me feel worse was if I had left one of my kids on that shuttle! Wild-eyed and panicked, I turned to a couple behind me in line.

"Can I please use your phone? I left mine on the shuttle." The wife quickly handed me her phone, and I punched in my cell number like a mad woman. I was prepared to beg the shuttle driver to turn around and return to the San Francisco airport. *Have mercy on me, sir,* I prayed silently. *Turn that van around.*

I waited through the second of silence while the numbers went through.

I nodded at the couple as if to say, "I got this. All cool."

And just like that, my bra started ringing.

I had tucked my precious phone in my bra just before I fell asleep on the shuttle. Don't ask me why — it was 3:00 a.m.! I had put my phone in my bra and gone to sleep, and after making a panicked scene in a crowded airport, I was holding a stranger's phone with my bra ringing. I wasn't the only one there to realize I was a mess.

The couple that had so generously loaned me their phone immediately smiled and looked away. I must have made a face of sheer horror standing there, listening to my ringing bra. Sheepishly, I handed them back

● ● ● ● ● ● ●

I HAD REACHED MY CAPACITY LEVEL AND WAS STANDING IN THE AIRPORT CALLING MY OWN BRA TO PROVE IT.

their phone. Who even knows what I said to them? As gracefully as was possible in a crowded airport line, I reached inside my bra and retrieved my phone.

I tried to look as if the whole entire thing was no big deal, but the heat and the color on my face told a much different story.

I had reached and surpassed my capacity level and was standing in the San Francisco airport calling my own bra to prove it.

Lessons from a Phone

Later, as I sat on the plane holding the culprit in my hand, I started laughing at the scene that replayed in my head. Oh, mercy, what a sight I must have been. Staring at my phone, I realized I had better get my crazy busy life under control, or I was going to have much bigger problems than a ringing bra.

Then, as I looked at my beloved iPhone, I realized it could teach me a thing or two about capacity.

As much as I love my phone, as much as I need what it can do, as awful as I feel when I am without it, I never ask my phone for more than it can give me. We have some great boundaries in our relationship, my phone and I.

I know exactly how much that phone has to offer. It has a limited capacity, and I respect that. It can only hold so much information and perform so many functions simultaneously. I know how much battery life it has left because it tells me in glowing numbers. And when the battery is low, the phone pings to warn me that I better find a power source. Ignore the warnings and … well, we all know the result.

Wouldn't life be so much easier if we each had a readout that told us, "This is your remaining capacity. Your energy reserves are low. Please stop and recharge"? Wouldn't it be great if we had some way to know where others were in terms of their capacity as well?

I don't know about you, but I think I'd love living in a world where people know and respect one another's capacity.

But we all know it's not that easy.

Capacity

It's easy to look at our phones and understand capacity.

- A phone runs off a battery that needs to be recharged or it will stop working.
- A phone has a finite capacity of storage and functionality.
- Different uses of the phone drain the battery at different rates.
- Each brand of phone is unique and operates differently.

Just as our phones have a certain capacity, we each have a unique capacity level. Our capacity depends on our personality, our experiences, and our seasons of life. People and events are constantly draining us, and we must recharge and off-load our excess or risk shutting down altogether.

Yet even though it's easy to see the correlation between our own capacity and that of a phone, we seem to lack the ability to find a reasonable rhythm, a sweet spot if you will, in a world of crazy busy.

Why is that? Why can't we choose not to be busy even when we know what lies ahead if we don't?

For one thing, I think as women we've convinced ourselves that being busy is a badge of honor. For example, have you noticed that whenever you ask someone how they are doing, instead of the old answer, "Fine," everyone's answer is now, "Good. Busy." Some have even nicknamed this the "busy-bragging" phenomenon.

According to Ray Williams, in *Psychology Today*, "In 2008, *USA Today* published a multi-year poll to determine how people perceived time and their own busyness. It found that each year, people reported that they were busier than the year before, with 69 percent responding that they were either 'busy,' or 'very busy.' Not surprisingly, women reported being busier than men, and those between ages thirty to sixty were the busiest. When the respondents were asked what they were sacrificing to their busyness, 56 percent cited sleep, 52 percent recreation, 51 percent hobbies, 44 percent friends, and 30 percent family."[1] For me, this research was comforting in an odd way. It showed me that I wasn't unusual at all. We are all dealing with similar struggles.

But I look at this survey and I think, "Okay, let me get this straight. Women are sacrificing sleep, recreation, hobbies, friends, and even family all at the altar of busyness. So we aren't sleeping, we aren't taking care of our bodies, and we aren't doing things we enjoy with people we love. Then what in the world are we busy doing?"

For me, it's easy to see that we need to get off the hamster wheel of crazy busy. Crazy busy is a life without peace. It's marked by decisions made for the approval of the world, not the approval of God. It's filled with what we think we "should" do, what we think will make others happy, and what we think being a good person (or good girl) looks like. All this busyness, in the end, keeps us just out of reach of the life we were created to live.

Any number of things can cause us to be crazy busy, and we'll be looking at many of those issues later in this book. Then we are going to tackle those things together. Not because I have a handle on breaking busy, but because I am working through it too. If I've learned anything in my life, it's that we are all in this thing together.

Crazy Busy

Have you ever said any of these things?

"I feel like I'm missing out on something, but I'm not sure
    what it is."
"I thought I would be happy when …"
"I'm so busy, but so is everyone else; it's just the way life is."
"I'm stressed. Everything is an emergency all the time."
"I thought doing so much for others would be fulfilling, but
    I just feel drained and empty."

If you are like me, you have said one, two, or maybe all those things at one time or another.

But what if I told you that you might be missing out on the life you are meant to live, missing out because you are operating in a world of crazy busy where the noise and distractions are keeping you from what you were meant to do?

How do I know this? I know because I have taken my own journey through the land of crazy busy, and it left me feeling how it has probably left you: tired, stressed, feeling empty and alone, hoping there is more to life than what you've been living.

A few years ago I found myself on the edge of burnout. My husband and I have five sons; yes, you heard that right, five sons. They range in age from kindergarten to high school. That means at any one time in our living room you may

STAYING BUSY WITH SHALLOW ACQUAINTANCES ONLY LEAVES US FEELING EMPTY.

see an ocean of Legos, a debate over who gets the iPad next, and sweaty football pads in a heap on the floor. It's loud, crazy, and requires way too much hand sanitizer.

I digress.

At the time of my near burnout, we both worked full-time. Mark worked at a hospital with normal human hours, and I ran my own business, which meant I worked all the time. We led a church small group, both taught on Sunday mornings, and my husband even coached peewee football.

From the outside, we must have looked like the all-American family (I'm sure it looked that way on Instagram, at least), just living the dream. But we were exhausted. We said yes to every request that came our way, not out of enthusiasm and joy, but out of guilt. We thought that was the way life had to be, and being "good" Christians meant we didn't say no. I mean, heaven forbid anyone should say we were (big dramatic pause) selfish.

One night, as we lay in bed, each of us quiet and lost in our own thoughts, I looked over at him, exhaled the longest, slowest sigh, and said, "I'm so done. I want to quit everything and run away. Maybe we could buy an RV and escape? You know, live off the land … well, except for gas … and Wi-Fi. You know what I mean? Let's just go. I can't take it anymore. I'm busier than I've ever been and feel worse about myself than I can remember ever feeling. I'm just done."

He laughed in that calm sort of way that men seem to be able to do and said, "You too?" He admitted he'd been hoping I was feeling that way (and would speak up soon), because he was feeling terrible about not enjoying our horrifically overscheduled weeks. He felt he "should" like everything he was doing, and he felt guilty that he didn't enjoy much of it at all anymore.

Mark's sigh matching mine, he rolled up on one elbow and looked down at me as he spoke. "Babe, all the things we are doing are good things, things people need us to help with. Like coaching. I say every year that I'll never coach again, but then they don't have anyone else, and I mean, someone has to do it, right?" (It's true. That did happen every single year, and every single year as he headed out the door to the parents' meeting I'd say, "Don't volunteer to coach. You know you don't want to do it." And every single year he'd yell back over his shoulder, "Don't worry, there is no way I'm volunteering this year. I'm a rock. No way I'm caving this time." But as soon as he walked back in the door, I'd know he'd volunteered again!)

He went on to say, "And it's all the other little things we do too. I mean, are any of the things we do things we want to do or are called to do, or are they all just things we feel like we have to do? I don't feel like I can catch my breath some days. It's exhausting."

I was relieved that we were both on the same page but grieved that we had let our lives get so crazy busy and out of control. Mark and I had reached (and surpassed) our capacity, ignoring all the warning signs along the way.

Maybe you've been there. Maybe you're there now.

The great news is, you *can* identify your capacity limits, find your sweet spot, and live beyond the world of crazy busy. In other words, you can *break* busy.

Signs of Capacity Overload

My granddaddy used to say, "If the Devil can't make you bad, he'll make you busy." That's some good Southern preacher wisdom right there.

I'll confess to you, before I broke busy in my own life, I proudly wore my busy badge of honor. I was the queen of busy. I even had the tiara and sash to go with it. Busyness made me feel productive and needed, and I easily overlooked the havoc it was wreaking in my life. Oh, there were warning signs, all kinds of them, but I just kept straightening my tiara and assuring myself I was a strong, confident woman, one who could handle the stress and chaos that had become my life.

But contrary to what many of us have been told, we all have limits. We can't handle it all, nor should we. We have to stop pretending we are superhuman with an endless supply of energy, because we aren't.

• • • • • •

EMBRACING OUR PERSONAL CAPACITY ALLOWS US TO LIVE OUT OUR CALLING.

So how do we know when we are reaching our limits? We aren't like our phones with flashing numbers that tell us we've reached our capacity. But there are signs our body gives us if we're paying attention, signs that may look different for each of us. For some the warning signs may be emotional. For others they might be physical, relational, or spiritual. But rest assured, if you are over capacity, you will soon find out — the hard way.

Sign #1: An Inability to Control Your Emotions

I was talking about reaching our limits with a leader at a large church recently. She shared that she can always tell when she's over capacity because she can no longer control her emotions. She told me this story:

I was scheduled to meet a group of friends for coffee. Alli, I love these women. They are my 'people.' But as I put on my mascara and thought through all the other things I should be doing that day, I realized I was beginning to dread it all. Within a few minutes, I went from looking forward to a relaxing morning with my girlfriends to feeling terribly anxious about the whole thing.

By the time I got to my car, I found myself feeling irritated and kinda angry with my friend who had set it all up. Didn't she realize how busy I was, how much I had on my plate? A real friend would have realized that the *last* thing I needed was one more thing to do.

About halfway there, I had worked myself into an anxious, angry mess. When I stopped at the next red light, I texted my friend and told her I wasn't going to be able to make it. I turned my car around and cried all the way home. I pulled into my garage and sat in the darkness, completely depressed. I convinced myself that if I could just get past this season of busyness, I'd be able to pull myself together. I'd be okay."

● ● ● ● ● ●

OUT-OF-CONTROL EMOTIONS OFTEN REFLECT THE OUT-OF-CONTROL DEMANDS WE PUT ON OURSELVES.

Doesn't that sound familiar? I have thought that same thing so many times. An inability to control our emotions and constantly feeling anxious, irritable, depressed, and overwhelmed are all signs that something isn't right. Out-of-control emotions often reflect the out-of-control demands we put on ourselves.

Sign #2: Lack of Self-Care

It's not fun to admit it, but I can totally relate to this one. People who operate at overcapacity rarely have time for self-care. I've often justified skipping a shower and working in my jammies all day because I had too much work to do. Or making Snickers and coffee my go-to meal because it was convenient and easy, despite the fact that it made me a caffeine-crazed maniac by the end of the day.

I find it easier to escape online than to take action for my own health and happiness. I've spent years goofing off on Pinterest and admiring other people's lives on Facebook instead of investing in my own life.

Maybe you've been there too? If we already have a full plate of obligations and crazy commitments, the last thing most of us want to do is spend time planning healthy meals, working out, or taking care of our physical health or appearance. That just sounds like more work.

But don't think you're alone if this describes you. The American Psychological Association released a study stating, "In general, Americans ... seem to understand the importance of healthy behaviors like managing their stress levels, eating right, getting enough sleep and exercise, but they report experiencing challenges practicing these healthy behaviors. They report being too busy."[2] When you start hearing yourself say things like "I'll rest when I'm dead," it might be time to take a look in the mirror and recognize this warning sign.

Taking care of yourself may seem selfish, but self-care is one of the most other-centered choices you can make in your life.

That's because you can't live the life God created you for, with space to be aware of his leading, if you don't take care of yourself. Self-care is never selfish.

Sign #3: Illness

There was a season in my life when I simply could not get well. I lived with a cold, a sinus infection, a stomach bug, or the flu almost all the time.

I remember telling a doctor once, "You have to help me. I am sick of being sick!"

He said, "Alli, is it possible you're stressed?"

I wanted to yell, "DUH!" but I restrained myself.

As I told him all the things in my life I had committed to or was responsible for, he said, "Alli, you're overloaded. As I see it, you've got a couple of choices: reduce your to-do list or stay sick."

Constant illness can be a sign of many things, and of course, you should see your doctor if you're struggling in this area. But illness can also be your body's warning to you that you need to make changes in your life.

(See what I did putting this section after self-care? A lack of self-care often leads to ongoing illness. I told you that self-care wasn't selfish!)

Sign #4: Chronic Lateness

I know I'm about to step on some toes here (mine most of all!), but I believe chronic lateness is caused by the tendency to say yes to too many activities and to too many people. It's a crazy cycle of trying to be all things to all people and to do more than is humanly possible. In the end, we can't get anywhere on time or accomplish everything we say we will, and we end up disappointing everyone because the weight of it is all too much.

A few years ago, I was at a large conference, waiting in the green room for my turn to speak. I was told someone named Robin would be assisting me that morning with anything I might need for my session, including a computer that had been set up with my presentation. No one had seen Robin yet, but the conference team told me not to worry because she was often late. "You'll recognize her right off," someone said. "She'll be the one carrying all the bags."

About forty minutes after I arrived, the woman I assumed must be Robin walked into the green room and greeted me with a great big smile. She had a baby on her back and was carrying three very large bags. One was a diaper bag (I assumed), and the other was filled with clothes, makeup, and hair products. The third bag looked like a computer bag, but the amount of files and paperwork sticking out of it left me doubtful that there was, in fact, a computer in there.

Robin introduced herself and excused her lateness and her appearance. She gave me a list a mile long of why she was late, how many obligations she had taken care of already that morning, and how busy she would be for the rest of the day.

Much to our horror, when Robin unpacked her computer bag, she realized she'd left my presentation PowerPoint, which I sent via email two weeks before, on her counter at home. She burst into tears and said, "I don't know why I even volunteered to work at this conference. I knew I didn't have time. I just didn't want to let anyone down."

I gave Robin a hug and told her that I thought she was superhuman for doing everything she was doing with a baby on her back, and I told her that if I had learned anything from years of giving presentations, it was to always have a backup presentation on a flashdrive. I pulled that little USB drive out of my purse, and we both started laughing out of relief.

I've known plenty of Robins in my day. I've *been* Robin so many times, and maybe you've been Robin too. How many times have we known we didn't have the time, energy, or emotional fortitude to put one more thing on our plates? How many times have we said yes out of obligation or guilt instead of out of genuine desire? For me, the answer is "too often," and that's one of the reasons I wanted to write these words, for you and me both! If you're noticing it is harder and harder to get anywhere on time and to accomplish things when you say you will accomplish them, it's probably a sign that you are over capacity.

Even though it seems easier to say yes to every demand and expect to be able to keep up, it's crucial to recognize that we all have limits. When you are over your limits, the right thing to do is to let someone who has capacity step in and run with it. You aren't letting anyone down. You are stewarding your time and energy well.

Sign #5: Self-Medicating and Excess

When the demands of life become too much, self-medicating is a very common response. For five years I ran a large women's conference, and it seemed everyone and everything needed my attention. There was always a problem to be solved, a speech to be made, sponsors who needed my attention, and decisions to make. It was endless. Once, a couple of close friends joked that they could always tell how stressed I was by how many times I touched up my makeup and how many Reese's Peanut Butter Cups I ate. To be honest, overeating sweets is a problem for me. It's something I have struggled with throughout my life. Anytime my life is out of balance, you can bet I'm probably curled up somewhere with a jar of Nutella and a spoon. I am absolutely a work in progress in many areas. This is one of them.

Self-medicating might also take the form of obsessive exercise, too many hours on social media, or watching a lot of television instead of getting much-needed sleep. Sometimes we can fool ourselves into thinking self-medicating is actually self-care — "I deserve that chocolate bar!" But if we find that our habits are directly related to stressful situations in our lives, and that they are not renewing or restoring us, then we need to recognize those choices as a warning sign of busyness. We need to ask ourselves if escaping reality just seems like an easier choice than reducing our to-do list.

Whether it is overindulging or a serious addiction, self-medicating is a serious warning sign. Left ignored, it can bring disaster to our lives.

Sign #6: Neglecting Important Relationships

Do any of these sound familiar?

- "You're always busy. You never have time for us anymore."
- "Do you have to check your email now? We're out to dinner."
- "This is the third time you've canceled our date."
- "Mom, can you please pick me up on time today? It's kind of embarrassing always being the last kid here."

Do you feel as if you are habitually letting down the people closest to you: your husband, children, close friends, family, and colleagues? It's easy to feel guilty about these things. And once we start feeling just a twinge of guilt, it's all over. The onslaught of pressure and guilt we heap on ourselves outweighs any positive feedback anyone else gives us. I've heard every single one of those statements above at one time or another and been in that painful loop of beating myself up over it.

When I begin neglecting my important relationships, I know I'm over capacity, and it's time to cut back to save my relationships and to save my peace of mind.

Sign #7: Neglecting God

In the Bible, we often see that Jesus is busy doing the work his Father sent him to do, living out his calling every day. But despite his very busy schedule, Jesus is undeterred from daily reconnecting with God. He leaves cities with people unhealed, prayers unprayed, and work undone all so he can spend time with God.

A huge sign that I am over capacity is when I start skipping church because I have too much to do, and I don't pray because I need to dive straight into work. Staying connected to God is what keeps me operating within my capacity and what helps me understand that God made me with limitations on purpose. Having a limited capacity is not a flaw in my character. It is by glorious design and for an incredible purpose: to realize my need for him.

Neglecting God out of our own busyness, combined with any of the other signs — lack of self-care, chronic lateness, illness, self-medicating, and neglecting our important relationships — are all symptoms that we are off balance. These are not things to beat ourselves up over, but they are signs we should heed.

Moses: The First Overworked Executive

Let's step back and take a look at what the Bible has to say about the crazy busy life. True, back then people didn't have cell phones, but neither did they have grocery stores, dishwashers, or store-bought clothes. Back then, just staying warm, fed, and clothed was enough to keep you crazy busy. Add to that any leadership duties, and you have a prescription for overload.

Just look at Moses. At one point he was living life in the desert of Midian, enjoying life with his wife and sons. Then God has him tell Pharaoh to let his people go, and Moses brings the Israelites out from under the rule of the Egyptians. His father-in-law, Jethro (whom I always imagine wearing overalls, because, c'mon, his name is JETHRO), himself a wise elder, comes to visit him and notices that Moses is living far above his capacity. He is serving as a judge for all of the people's issues. He has people before him all day long, and he singlehandedly has to solve all their issues. Can you imagine? I get exhausted just thinking about it.

Moses' father-in-law comments,

> What you are doing is not good. You and these people who come to you will only wear yourselves out. The work is too heavy for you; you cannot handle it alone. Listen now to me and I will give you some advice, and may God be with you. You must be the people's representative before God and bring their disputes to him. Teach them his decrees and instructions, and show them the way they are to live and how they are to behave. But select capable men from all the people — men who fear God, trustworthy men who hate dishonest gain — and appoint them as officials over thousands, hundreds, fifties and tens. Have them serve as judges for the people at all times, but have them bring every difficult case to you; the simple cases they can decide themselves. That will make your load lighter, because they will share it with you. If you do this and God so commands, you will be able to stand the strain, and all these people will go home satisfied. (Exodus 18:17–23)

Moses was operating far above his physical capacity, and Jethro had to tell him to check himself before he wrecked himself (as the kids would say). Moses had to learn to delegate his work:

"But select capable men from all the people — men who fear God, trustworthy men who hate dishonest gain — and appoint them as officials over thousands, hundreds, fifties and tens" (v. 21). Without delegation of his workload, Moses would burn himself out and not be the leader of his people that God created him to be.

Just as Moses had limits, we too have limits on what we take on. "Doing it all" isn't biblical. The world says we must do it all, but God says we must do only what he gives us to do. (We'll talk more about this later in the book.) This means abandoning the never-ending need to please.

The belief that we can and "should" do it all ourselves is a lie that haunts us. When you feel the weight of trying to do it all, just remember Jethro (imaginary overalls and all) and get yourself some help.

Embracing What Limits Our Capacity

Understanding the warning signs of capacity overload is important. But we also have to be aware of and embrace what affects our capacity. Sometimes it's not just *what* we are doing but *when* and *why* we are doing it that affects us.

1. Identify your season of life

Different seasons of life affect our capacity. Times of huge stress — such as a move, a marriage, a divorce, a new job, a new baby, or serious illness — drain our energy supply more quickly. We might know that in theory, but sometimes when we're going through those times, we forget that we may not have the capacity we used to have or that we *want* to have.

When Mark and I realized we were living well beyond our capacity limits, every single thing we were doing was great. We just couldn't handle all those things all at the same time in the season of life we were in — running a business, raising five sons ages three to thirteen, and moving to a new house. Any one of those things could have drained our capacity. So it's no wonder that in the middle of *that* season, my infamous ringing bra incident happened.

How would you describe the season you're in right now? Sometimes writing down your current circumstances, or telling them to a friend, helps us recognize how much we have going on just in our households and workplaces, let alone the things that get added on.

Embracing the season of life we are in and the limitations that come with it helps us break busy and live life at a saner, more sustainable pace.

2. Identify your stress points

I am not naturally a morning person. I have come to terms with this. For years, doing something early in the morning was pretty much a recipe for disaster with me. I won't say I've done worse than the bra-ringing incident, but let's just leave it at, "I'm not naturally a morning person." Now that I understand this about myself and have identified it as one of my stress points, I'm careful not to schedule anything before 8 a.m. It's that simple.

I have also learned I'm not a toddler person anymore. I was a toddler person when my boys were young, but looking back on it now, I realize how exhausting those years really were. (If you are reading this with a toddler dumping juice on your lap, trying to stick their fingers in an uncovered outlet, and dumping all the contents of your drawers on the floor, God bless you, sister. It does get easier and you will be able to relax again, I promise!) The thought of having to take care of a toddler drains me just to think about. Put it this way: if asked to volunteer in a church toddler room, I'm first to run out the door.

But teenagers, I'm awesome with teenagers. Teenagers don't suck my capacity dry the way toddlers do. This doesn't make me a bad person. There are plenty of people out there who are better with toddlers than with teenagers. We offset each other.

The fact that certain circumstances and certain people drain our capacity is important information. It lets us set proper limitations on what we do, when we do it, and with whom we do it.

3. Identify why you are exceeding your capacity

If you already know your own limits, why do you sometimes exceed them? Here I believe a little soul-searching comes in handy. For instance, when I spend time in self-reflection, I find that pride often gets in the way of me saying no to commitments that stretch my capacity. Had I been honest about my lack of ability to handle a 6:00 a.m. flight, I could have avoided the whole stress of "losing" my phone! I needed to kill my pride and be okay to tell some people no (including myself). Instead, I wanted to get as much done as possible that day and not let anyone down (including myself!).

In addition to pride, any number of things can cause us to exceed our capacity. We might be too focused on "getting ahead." We might be operating outside of our area of giftedness. We might be making bad decisions based on guilt or people pleasing. We might be caught up in perfectionism. Stepping back to evaluate *why* we are doing what we are doing gives us insights into whether or not we need to keep doing them.

Limited versus Limitless Capacity

When God created us, he created us with a limitless capacity to love others and a limitless ability to stretch our talents to be used for his glory. He also created us with a body that needs rest, and he placed us in a universe that has a limited number of hours in each day. When we operate under the belief that we can do it all, we're forgetting how God wants us to rely on him. We're adding so much extra "noise" to our lives that we can't hear his voice speaking our true calling. God may, indeed, be calling us to coach the football team or teach Sunday school or run our own business. But if we don't have times of quiet in our lives, we'll miss hearing what to say yes to and what to say no to.

Jesus made us a promise: "Come to me, all you who are weary and burdened, and I will give you rest. Take my yoke upon you and learn from me, for I am gentle and humble in heart, and you will find rest for your souls. For my yoke is easy and my bur-

> •••••••
> **JESUS PROMISES US A SPIRITUAL SWEET SPOT EVEN WITHIN THE WORLD OF CRAZY THAT SURROUNDS US.**

den is light" (Matthew 11:28–30). That isn't to say that our lives will be easy with Jesus. But he promises us a spiritual sweet spot even within the world of crazy that surrounds us.

Learning to Recharge

Breaking busy is about more than identifying the things in our life that suck the life out of us. We must also identify what gives us life, what recharges us and restores our capacity.

When Mark and I made our declaration that we were breaking busy, we both decided to be purposeful in spending our time in ways that recharged us. I decided I would like to unwind at the end of the day by hanging out on Facebook. But I soon realized that my time on social media was draining me instead of recharging me. I realized that I spent so much of my work life online that anytime I went online, my brain clicked into "work mode."

I was surprised at the things that actually did recharge me and restored my capacity. Quiet music and solitude recharged me, but spending time with my family, snuggling the little guys before bed, and reading while snuggled up to my husband as he watched football also restored me.

As I have talked with other women while writing this book, I have been surprised at how different we are with regard to what drains us and what gives us life. (I have a friend who dreads the process of putting all the kids to bed and can't believe snuggling with the little guys at bedtime restores me — it would exhaust her!) We each have a different capacity level. Our levels increase and decrease, depending on our season and our situation. Finding our own sweet spot in a world of crazy will take self-awareness, self-discipline, and a super dose of the Holy Spirit guiding us along the way.

Life in Your Sweet Spot

We've talked about what drains us and what restores us. Now let's tackle what life looks like when we live in our sweet spot. By "sweet spot," I don't mean a place where life is easy and we chill with our feet up all day. Life is full of challenges, and those challenges are what enable us to grow and lead richer, fuller lives. Everyone who is dedicated to living out their God-given destiny is called to grow and stretch, and growth isn't always comfortable, even within our true sweet spot.

Our true sweet spot is the place where we know we are

operating at our best. My iPhone's sweet spot is when it is plugged in, charged, and has a strong Wi-Fi connection. It has no unnecessary apps in the background draining the batteries or thousands of pictures slowing it down.

My sweet spot is making choices each day to eat well and get enough sleep, take care of my most important relationships, and, most importantly, plug in to the ultimate power source: God through the Holy Spirit.

Don't miss this. Our sweet spots aren't meant to be areas in which our lives are perfect (because perfect is a lie, and we'll unpack more on that later!). Operating in our true sweet spot means we are taking care of the big things — God, loved ones, and ourselves — so that we have a solid foundation to live out our calling in this world of crazy.

Action Steps

1. Your phone battery tells you its remaining capacity on a scale of 0–100 percent. Using that same scale, what is your capacity right now?

2. Are there any warning signs in your life that indicate you are close to the end of your capacity? What are they?

3. Too many photos and too many apps can clutter up your phone, drain the battery, and reduce its capacity. In the same way, too many activities or possessions can clutter up your life, drain your emotional reserves, and reduce your capacity to live in God's calling. What are the things you might need to discard to regain some capacity in your life?

4. What recharges you? In Luke 6, Jesus retreats from the crowds and his disciples to be in solitude with God. What is the time and place in your life where you can get away from the busy of life in order to be alone with God?

5. What does living in your sweet spot look like?

TWO

RELATIONSHIPS

*Finding Your Connection in a
World of Acquaintances*

I met Mark on a blind date in a Cajun restaurant in Knoxville, Tennessee. From the moment I saw him, I knew he was the one for me. But never, and I mean never, did I imagine that we would end up on an adventure that would include five boys, eight moves, and losing everything we owned and building it all back again. I mean, when we dream of getting married, we think of holding hands and skipping through a meadow whispering sweet nothings, right? Oh, how the scenes in romantic comedies spoil our perspective on what real romance is like.

I was barely in my twenties when I met Mark. My friend Jennifer had all but insisted that I let her set me up with her friend from work because it was apparent to everyone (sigh) that I had made terrible choices in guys over the past few years. Mark had dark hair and glasses, and I could tell from ten feet away he was comfortable in his own skin. He was smart, sincere, and self-confident. Over dinner he told me stories of safaris in Africa (I had been fascinated with Africa since I was a little girl!), his love of Shakespeare, and his obsession with the Pittsburgh Steelers. I was smitten despite the fact that Shakespeare gave me a headache, and I wasn't sure I'd ever heard of the Steelers before. There was something special about this man, and deep in my soul, I knew I could (and would) listen to the sound of his voice for the rest of my life.

Six months later, on a sticky August day in the mountains of East Tennessee, we tied the knot. My paternal granddaddy, a retired minister, performed our ceremony. Mark was almost nine years my senior, enough time for a man to mature and catch up with the maturity of women, I said smugly. As Forrest Gump would say, "We fit together like peas and carrots."

Getting Busy and Striving Hard

I threw myself into marriage to Mark and devoted myself to being the "perfect" wife and stepmom to his daughter, Jessica. I had my white-picket-fence life all planned out. Of course, I didn't realize it at the time, but my desire for a June Cleaver-esque life and a big, happy family was born out of my own painful past. My father died suddenly in a car accident when I was two and a half years old, and my mother married a man who wasn't exactly ready to be a good dad. So I was set on creating the family I had always wanted. While Mark worked outside of our home, I spent the next ten years busy with pregnancies, breastfeeding, and toddler chaos.

As a hospital administrator who specialized in turning failing laboratories around, Mark's job required us to move to new cities (or states) every two years. In fact, all five of our boys were born in different cities. We were busy in the craziest kind of way. Babies, moves, cardboard boxes, toddlers, and road maps all filled my twenties.

Finally, after spending ten years hop-scotching from Florida to Rhode Island, New York, Ohio, and Maryland, I was overjoyed when Mark got a job in my beloved home state of Tennessee. My feet were planted in soil I knew and loved, and Mark and I both felt we finally could put down some roots. We were living the dream. Our two-story brick house had fancy granite countertops and bathrooms with dual sinks. Gone were my childhood days of oversized hand-me-downs when I was ashamed to have friends over, too embarrassed for them to see where I lived. We had arrived.

But without warning, six months after we settled in, Mark's job ended. It just ended. The news was a sucker punch to us both. We were left dizzy and confused, wondering what was next for our family. Because our fifth son, Jeremiah, was on the way, I begged Mark not to move us to a new part of the country. The thought of packing up and unpacking again was just too overwhelming. More than that, I loved my house. It's not easy to admit this, but I realize now that I wanted to stay put because, by the world's standards, we had made it. My massive pride was planted on the mantel of the home Mark and I had built. And let me tell you, when your pride is as big as mine was, there's pretty much only one direction to go. I was not only ungrateful to God for our home, I all but ignored him in my daily life. I was too busy for him, and he was about to let my choices break me.

Losing Everything

Of course, like so many people, our version of "made it" involved lots of debt and a house and cars with crazy high payments. There was no cushion of savings for emergencies. We lived way beyond our means because we knew there would always be another paycheck. But when Mark lost his job, we had to put our dream house up for sale. And with very little time to sell our house and very few buyers in the market, we found ourselves in the midst of foreclosure and then bankruptcy.

We lost everything at the very beginning of the financial crisis. I can laughingly say now, "We lost everything before losing everything was cool," but at the time it wasn't so funny. Five weeks after our youngest was born, we had to face reality. It was time to stop pretending that everything would be okay.

We rented two storage pods and kept only what would fit in them. Everything else went to friends, Goodwill, or was thrown away. It's funny what possessions you realize have meaning in those moments. The clothes I spent so much money on were given away, but I kept the box of toys that would make the boys feel more secure whenever and wherever we finally unpacked them. The expensive appliances were donated and the photo albums stayed. The crystal wine glasses were given away, and the glider rocker that I rocked and nursed my babies in over the last decade remained.

We had placed our hopes and trust in possessions and worldly pursuits, and now everything we trusted in was gone. Too late I learned the lesson that Jesus taught: "Do not store up for yourselves treasures on earth, where moths and vermin destroy, and where thieves break in and steal [*and where banks giveth, and banks taketh away*]. But store up for yourselves treasures in heaven, where moths and vermin do not destroy, and where thieves do not break in and steal [*and where banks can't call a debt and foreclose*]. For where your treasure is, there your heart will be also" (Matthew 6:19–21, words in italics added, obviously).

My heart had definitely been in the wrong place.

Love > Possessions

We lost our possessions, our treasures, things we had strived for and placed so much value in, only to discover they had no value at all. In his loving mercy, God showed me the beauty in the ashes of my life. He allowed me to see it was not *the things* I strived for (home, appearance of success) that gave me real peace, purpose, and happiness, but the relationships I had with those I loved.

If we are going to start breaking busy, we start with focusing in on the relationships that fill our soul. Breaking busy means breaking the idea that keeping up with the Joneses will ever bring us any peace in this world. The relentless desire to acquire worldly security or position can sometimes be the thing that brings us down. That's why Jesus told us to have a different mindset:

> Therefore I tell you, do not worry about your life, what you will eat or drink; or about your body, what you will wear. Is not life more than food, and the body more than clothes?... So do not worry, saying, "What shall we eat?" or "What shall we drink?" or "What shall we wear?" For the pagans run after all these things, and your heavenly Father knows that you need them. But seek first his kingdom and his righteousness, and all these things will be given to you as well. (Matthew 6:25, 31–33)

Over the years we rebuilt our finances, and now we live in a beautiful home again. But we learned to live and work with our priorities firmly rooted in our faith, with our focus on God. We've tried to seek God's will first, obeying him, and thanking him for the blessings he gives us.

What I ultimately learned in losing everything is that my relationship with God is the most important thing in my life, and my relationships with my spouse and others are the key to a successful, happy life. Instead of running after "all these things," I've learned to walk with God, loving him and others along the way.

Learning to (Finally) Turn to God

After we left our dream home, we didn't know where we would end up. We were officially homeless, humble, and scared of what was next. God had broken our busy striving and finally had our attention. I gave in, reluctantly, to the reality that a new job in Nashville wasn't happening and agreed that Mark should accept job interviews in faraway states. In the meantime, I convinced the kids we were going on a fun vacation as we headed for the home of my maternal grandfather in the mountains of East Tennessee.

At night, Mark and I lay in bed together, holding hands and praying. Over the course of the next few weeks, God revealed to us where we had gone off track. We were worshiping the false idols of success and money, and we had forgotten where our hope came from.

By the fifth week at my grandfather's, Mark had been across the country twice for interviews, and I had become almost happy about the possibility of moving to Podunkville, USA, in the middle of nowhere, because we just needed a way out of the mess we had ourselves in.

Late one night, before we fell asleep, I turned to Mark and said, "Just let me sell my wedding ring. We need the money." With his eyes full of tears he said, "Don't do that to me. Don't ever say it again." His heart was broken. We were a mess. In life, when we admit what messes we really are, God can finally mold us, like clay in the potter's hand, into what he created us to be and who we are meant to be in him.

The next night, while holding hands with tears falling down around us, we prayed a prayer of complete trust. "Lord, we've spent too long focused on what we wanted. We've lived for too long by our own rules. Forgive us for our pride and greed. Rescue us from the mess we have ourselves in. We give our lives to you in whatever way that means. Take us and have your way with us. We are yours."

One of the most amazing things about God is that we really can have a relationship with him through Jesus Christ. He listens, he forgives, he rescues those who call him Lord. He heard our cry that night, and he knew our hearts were honest, our stiff necks softened, and our selfishness subdued.

The very next week Mark received a call from a hospital outside Nashville. As he prepared to drive back to Nashville for the interview, I cried in relief. He cautioned me, "Babe, I don't have the job yet. It's just an interview. I've been on lots of interviews in the last few weeks. Don't get your hopes so high yet." There was no dampening my hopes though. I knew we were going home to Nashville, but I also knew our lives would be different. This time we would live a life given over to God — not in our strength, not in our wisdom, but relying on God and God alone. And that is exactly what happened.

Connection with God

I think that sometimes we Christians forget how special it is that we can have a relationship, a real, close, personal relationship with God.

What stands out about the Christian life, compared to all other religions, is the fact that we can have a personal relationship with a living God through Jesus Christ and the Holy Spirit.

I was reading *Jesus Calling* by Sarah Young this summer when I came across this entry. (In case you aren't familiar with her devotional guide, it is written from the point of view of God speaking to us.)

I speak to you continually. My nature is to communicate, though not always in words. I fling glorious sunsets across the sky, day after day after day. I speak in the faces and voices of loved ones. I caress you with a gentle breeze that refreshes and delights you. I speak softly in the depths of your spirit, where I have taken up residence.

You can find me in each moment, when you have eyes that see and ears that hear. Ask my Spirit to sharpen your spiritual eyesight and hearing. I rejoice each time you discover my presence. Practice looking and listening for me during quiet intervals. Gradually you will find Me in more and more of your moments. You will seek Me and find Me, when you seek Me above all else.[3]

It is the most incredible thing to me that the God of the universe, my God, speaks to me continually. The same God who spoke me into existence. Who spoke the world into motion. He speaks to *me*.

And he waits for me to connect with him. But sometimes, setting aside the busyness of life to connect with him can be overwhelming. The call to break busy and nurture our relationship with him is real and necessary — not just finding time, but *making time* to stay connected. Here are three great ways I have found to help me stay connected to God:

1. Prayer

When our kids were little, we used to teach them that prayer was simply talking to God. To a certain extent, that is true. But prayer is a conversation, and a conversation is a two-way street. It's about talking and listening. When I pray, I don't use a formula, per se, but I do try to make it more than just throwing out my list of needs and wants.

I think of praying as unhurried time with the Lord. I praise him. I thank him. And I sit in silence and listen to what he wants for me and from me. I am not afraid to ask God for anything. First John 5:14 tells us, "This is the confidence we have in approaching God: that if we ask anything according to his will, he hears us." I have come to learn that prayer is about so much more than asking God for things. It is an intimate conversation between my Maker and me.

2. Reading the Bible

Years ago, a mentor encouraged me to read a chapter of Proverbs each day. Proverbs has thirty-one short chapters, so reading a chapter a day over the course of a month was easy. Even though I've been reading the same proverbs over and over again each month since then, I still read them and think, *Wow, I never noticed that one before like that.* God's Word is continually new to us because it speaks to us through the filter of the circumstance of life we are in.

My mentor taught me the SPECKS method, which she created to help people learn to read the Bible. As I read a chapter of the Bible, I ask God these questions:

> *Is there a . . .*
> **S**in to avoid?
> **P**romise to claim?
> **E**xample to follow?
> **C**ommand to obey?
> **K**nowledge of God to acquire?
> **S**ummary for the day?

Asking myself these questions helps me set aside the clutter in my mind and focus on what God wants to say to me.

3. Worship

On some of my worst days, when I've not known what to pray, the act of worship brings me back to the place I need to be. Often I sing in my car. (Mind you, I'm the world's worst singer. When I sing I make a painful, not joyful noise.) And in the morning, after the kids are off to school, I pour a cup of coffee and sing along with my favorite worship playlist. Just the act of singing along in worship is life-giving. It strengthens me, settling my mind on God and his goodness.

It wasn't until the last few years that I fell in love with worship time at church. I think I used to be too distracted or focused on myself. Thoughts like, *My Spanx are too tight*, or *Where will we go after church*, or *I hope Jeremiah isn't crying in the nursery*, used to keep me self-focused instead of focused on the actual act of worship.

But these days, when the whole sanctuary is worshiping together and the presence of the Lord comes in such a powerful way, tears roll down my cheeks. Every time. Mark has learned that I'm okay even when I tear up during the service. The older boys stopped getting embarrassed by me long ago. I can't tell you enough how much I love worshiping with the body of believers. Luckily my church plays the music loud so my joyful noises don't ruin everyone else's worship time. Because my joyful noises really would. I promise.

Where True Love and Real Life Meet

The picture of true love most of us have in our minds rarely matches the picture of real life. And often it is where the "idea" of true love and the reality of married life meet that marriages break down. When Mark and I were dating, I told him I dreamed of having five kids one day. I think he secretly thought he could change my mind but, as luck would have it, those five kids came, mixed in with some heartbreaking miscarriages as well. We learned that we had to break busy and stay connected to each other if we had a shot at making our crazy, less-than-picturesque lives work. My husband and I found our love for each other and our connectedness and strength through our years of struggle. From lost babies to lost homes to lost dreams — the shared struggles are what brought us together so deeply. What I've learned is that a great marriage isn't made of moments you see in the movies — luxury locations, fancy surroundings, and material wealth. Marriages are made in moments of weakness, humility, and instability. In those moments, two people either pull together or get torn apart, and by God's grace and our determination, Mark and I pulled together.

Trust me when I tell you, it is no small miracle that Mark and I have survived the trials of our life. Not only has it required us individually and jointly to stay connected to God, it has also required us to stay connected to each other. Between work, kids, and a gazillion sports practices, we have to fight to break busy and stay connected to each other.

I grew up watching romantic comedies and dreaming of being swept off my feet daily in marriage, but the sweetest, most meaningful moments in my marriage rarely occur in those romantic comedy sorts of ways. Sometimes they occur late at night after the kids all go to sleep and we are left holding hands with a deep relaxed sigh before we drift off to sleep. And sometimes they occur as we catch each other's eye across a room and laugh as we give each other that knowing look, "These boys are driving us crazy! How are we going to survive until bedtime?"

For Mark and me, one of the easiest ways to stay connected

is by sharing our daily "wins" or highlights. If you've ever seen the highlight reel on ESPN, you know what I'm talking about.

Staying connected at the end of the day can be as easy as giving each other a few key highlights of the day. It keeps us connected, in tune with what is going on in each other's lives and able to celebrate each other's wins.

● ● ● ● ● ●

STRONG MARRIAGES ARE MADE OF COUPLES WHO UNDERSTAND THAT STAYING CONNECTED IS MORE IMPORTANT THAN STAYING BUSY.

And can we get real for a minute? No book that talks about real connection with your husband can leave out sex. I know many of us grew up thinking of sex as bad, so when we got married we still felt a little guilty about enjoying it. I'm here to tell you that having and enjoying sex with your husband is the number one way to stay connected in the good times and the bad.

Researchers have identified a scary fact: If couples don't have sex at least once a month, it is a strong indicator of marital unhappiness and (yikes) impending divorce.[4] When Mark and I were engaged, a counselor told me, "Honey [we all call each other honey in the South, don't ya know?], be sure to have lots of sex. Ladies need it to feel loved, men need it to feel connected. God designed you both to need it, have it, and love it." At the time I nodded blankly, trying to wrap my brain around the fact that, in a crowded restaurant, she just told me to have lots of sex (my Southern sensibilities were in shock)! But it was some of the best advice anyone ever gave me.

Whether it's sharing the bed or sharing the highlights of the day, work on staying connected to your spouse. And yes, sometimes breaking busy means getting naked and letting yourself have fun!

Carving Out Time in a Full Day

Every night at 8:00 p.m., the kids' bedtime routine begins. The three youngest guys brush their teeth and try to beat each other to bed. Why? Because when you get to bed first in this house, you get snuggled first. No one likes to wait for snuggle time. Snuggle time is when I snuggle up with one of them at a time, we listen to a song or two on my iPhone (normally worship songs, Disney songs, or, if it's between Thanksgiving and New Year's — a Christmas song), we read a short book, and we talk about the day. I always insist on hearing three things that they are grateful for, or at least three things they were happy about that day. It may sound simple, coming up with three things each night, but like every other practice, it is a discipline, just like Mark and me connecting each day to discuss our wins.

We laugh, we talk about the day, and I always have to remind the other brothers that they need to "respect their brother's snuggle time" and hush up until it's their snuggle time. I'm worn out after tucking in kids for an hour, but the daily routine of snuggle time has proven to be an investment with huge returns for us all.

Our relationship with our kids is enriched by the daily practice of doing life together. Just a few minutes of one-on-one, discussing the day or sharing a funny moment from school, gives us that chance to make a connection. In those focused moments kids feel safe and can share if there is a fear or a struggle they need help with. No kid throws down a backpack and says, "Hi, Mom, I'm hungry. And I'm struggling with where I fit in with my friends and feeling unsure of myself. Can you help me figure this out?" Yeah, not going to happen. But carving out those focused minutes gives kids the chance and space to bring up issues as they feel comfortable. I daily have to break the cycle of busy and decide to invest in that special connection time with the kids.

Finding Connection with Friends

Husbands are great. Kids are great. Parents and siblings are great. But no matter how great your relationships are with all these people — you need your girlfriends. You need a couple chicks who will love you enough to tell you that you look ridiculous in those skinny leather pants, that you really were being a jerk at the office, or they understand the struggle you are going through.

When I asked women on Facebook why they don't spend more time pouring into their friendships, I heard these things:

- We just moved to a new town; I haven't made any real connections yet.
- Who has time to go sit and drink coffee and chitchat? I have so much to do!
- My best friend from college and I moved to different states, and it's exhausting to think about starting over.

Over the past twenty years, one study showed that our circle of close friends and confidants is rapidly declining. Eighty percent of people said they talk only to family members about important matters. Almost 10 percent of people talk only to their spouse about personal issues, and only 15 percent of folks have four or five close confidants.[5]

I can't imagine how much pressure this puts on married couples to bear the burden of being the key person in each other's lives for stability, finances, raising children, and almost all the emotional support for each other. In fact, research shows that we put a strain on our marriages by expecting our spouse to satisfy more needs than any one person can actually meet.[6]

In my life, my friends have taken a lot of the emotional burden off my husband. Mark is my best friend, my soul mate, and the one person on this earth who knows me best, but he would prefer not to have to hear detailed rundowns every day of exactly what happened and how I feel about each thing. You know who does? My girlfriends. I know if I want to talk about life in general, I call Megan. If I want to talk about marriage or what God is showing me in my life, I call Carol. If I want to talk about business strategies, I call Rachel. If I'm worried I am a bad mom because I lost my temper and yelled at the boys, I call Colleen. If I want to talk about Jesus while at the same time admitting that I hate *everything* in my closet and don't know what to wear, I call Bianca. Now, don't think Mark doesn't still know about it all; I just give him the concise update on things after I've gone over every last detail with my girls.

My mom gave me a piece of advice that has been so good for my marriage: "Baby, don't treat your man like he's your girlfriend. Let your best friend be your girlfriend and let your husband be your man. You won't be disappointed, and he will be so happy being who he really is."

True friends celebrate with you on the best of days and build you up on your worst days. And sometimes they speak hard truths into your life because they love you enough to not let you be a terrible person. But for me, the best measurement I have for a true friend? They pour life into me instead of draining it out.

• • • • • •
OUR CALLING IS NOT TO KEEP TRYING TO WIN OVER THE JERKS.

This doesn't mean we always need to be on the quest for the "perfect" friend — we will never find her and we will never *be* her! But our calling is not to keep trying to win over the jerks. Love them, pray for them, but don't waste your time trying to get them to love you. It's a battle you are guaranteed to lose.

Keeping true connections in your life and not allowing

negative people to drain you dry will help you break busy. Why? Because you will be spending your precious time on your most important relationships, those that fill you up instead of drain the life out of you.

Real Relationships in an Era of Social Media

We can't talk about relationships without diving into the topic of social media. Do social media sites — Facebook, Instagram, Twitter — help us stay authentically connected, or do they fill our lives with lots of loose connections based on acquaintances? Like everything in life, it depends on how you use them. Research shows that the more we use Facebook and other forms of social media as a passive participant — scrolling through news feeds and Instagram images — the more loneliness and sadness we feel.[7] Using technology to replace face-to-face friendships is where we can get off track. We can waste countless hours busying ourselves with something that doesn't fill our souls.

I love social media. Love it. Love the fact that I can stay connected to people all over the world, love that I can see my friends' babies' smiles across town or across the globe, love that I can share my life and let others in that way. But over the past couple of years, I made the decision not to be online all day long. I reached the point where scrolling through Facebook left me feeling disconnected with friends and family, not connected. *I need more time with my face looking at others' faces in real life and less time looking at Facebook*, I decided. No matter how many likes I got on that well-crafted picture that makes life look perfect, unless my real relationships at home and with Christ are strong, no number of likes and comments will fill my heart.

Technology can help us connect with others if we use it intentionally. The key is to be actively engaged instead of passively scrolling through other people's highlight-reel moments. Most importantly, use technology to help schedule in more face-to-face time, because only that investment of time and energy will build the bonds of real connection.

Deeply connected relationships are the key for happiness and fulfillment in life. The world's benchmarks for success are the things that can disappear in an instant, but real success in life is found through a connection to Christ and the

• • • • • •
UNLESS OUR REAL RELATIONSHIPS AT HOME AND WITH CHRIST ARE STRONG, NO NUMBER OF LIKES AND COMMENTS WILL FILL OUR HEARTS.

ability to give and receive love from others. If we are going to start breaking busy, we have to focus on the relationships that fill our soul and not just the ones that fill our calendar.

Action Steps

1. Ask yourself: What are the things in my life that truly matter?

2. How can you deepen your connection to Christ? What one thing can you do each day to build your connection?

3. Pick one thing that will connect you more deeply to an important person in your life — then do it.

THREE

CALLING

Finding Your Purpose in a World of Striving

The years of raising young kids and trying to be June Cleaver all blurred together like the landscape on a long car trip. Bits and pieces of memories stick out, like roadside attractions in the journey of parenting a big family: the world's biggest diaper blowout in public (the time I forgot to pack extra baby clothes, and I had to fly cross-country with a baby wearing just a diaper because he blew out his "travel outfit." Whoops!), worst reason to visit the ER (old pinto bean in a nostril), or most embarrassing reason to apologize to your neighbors (your sons fished koi out of their backyard pond).

In those early years, I was busy doing so much helicopter parenting and striving to be such a great homemaker that somewhere along the way, I lost myself. I was Mark's wife, Jessica's stepmom, Justin, Jack, and Joey's mom (James and Jeremiah came later) — but as for me? I was a robot serving needs, never even giving God time to whisper to me who I was in him. I had people to please, decorating to do, and kids to teach. There was no time to sit and talk to God! And so the years blurred by.

The winter of 2006 seemed especially brutal in western New

York. My husband and I were visiting his parents for Christmas, and I had escaped on the fresh snowplowed streets to the local bookstore to wander the aisles. Out of nowhere, I began day-dreaming about writing a book. The thought seemed crazy. I was never great at school. My grammar horrified my English teachers. I was a mom of three boys with a lifetime of bad decisions to my credit. What business did I have thinking I could write a book? I shook my head and laughed at myself.

But on the long drive back to Narragansett, Rhode Island, where we lived at the time, one question ran through my mind over and over: *What do I have to say?* The miles of white, snow-covered hills flattened, and by the time we reached the shore, getting the boys and the suitcases into the house overtook any thoughts I had of writing.

But a few weeks later, I braved the painfully slow dial-up and did what anyone with a dream does. I Googled it. As the dial-up connection screeched, I entered into the search engine: "How do you publish a book?" The results were depressing. Apparently if I wasn't famous, infamous, or well-networked, publishing a book was a no-go. *Well, shoot. I'm not any of those things*, I thought.

I kept searching and read that another way to publish a book was to build a popular blog and show publishers that you have something to say to an audience who wants to hear it. *Hmmm.*

Of course, my next search was "What is a blog?"

It took a year and another son (the fourth, if you are counting) to start that first blog. I guess it did take me a while to figure out what I wanted to say to the world, but I finally decided I would write about what I knew: my family, topics that I was interested in, like current events, and faith.

I called it Mrs. Fussypants because that was Mark's nickname for me. Can you just imagine how infuriating it is when you are mad and your husband sings, "She's Mrs. Fussypants. Stay outta her way." Yeah, I wish I had thought of a classier name. Who knew anyone would actually read it? But read it they did.

The blog started a little after the creation of Twitter. For this intellectually bored, relatively lonely (don't forget we moved to a new state every couple of years) woman, the ability to connect with others in a new way energized me. I loved reading the stories of other women's lives. I found great comfort in knowing I wasn't alone in the daily struggles of marriage, parenting, and faith. Their stories gave me hope. They made me laugh. They distracted me from what was often a very mundane life. When my babies were sleeping, or we couldn't leave the house because everyone had some awful flu virus, my blog and Twitter conversations with people around the world allowed me to feel not quite so trapped and alone. Blogging sparked something inside of me, a renewed passion for helping other people by sharing things I'd learned. It was one of the first times I discovered that becoming busy doing something I loved could actually be a form of breaking busy in the rest of my life. It was busy with a purpose — a purpose that started in childhood.

A Passion Awakened

When I was a ten-year-old girl, I used to check out as many books as the librarian would let me (which was twenty-five, if you are wondering). I was so hungry to discover the world, and those books opened it up to me. I loved sharing what I learned with my family. They often (through many eye rolls and sighs) told me that my "gift" was keeping people well-informed. Of course I knew they were joking, and probably being very sarcastic, but I did think that learning and sharing what I had learned was a gift. At the very least, it was something I was passionate about.

When my blogging reawakened that passion, I was relentless

in my desire to learn new things and share them with others. I stopped being so busy trying to impress the other moms in whatever playgroup I was in at the time (which made me miserable) and got busy fulfilling a mission I felt called to.

I had no connections, no special abilities, no real idea what I was doing. What I had on my side was the desire to figure out life and share what I was learning with others. I was curious, just brave enough to dip my toes in the online waters, and dumb enough to try. With the encouragement and help of a group of online friends, I launched an online magazine called *Blissfully Domestic*, which I thought would take the Internet by storm. Of course, that was before Martha Stewart and her friends all decided to go digital too. (Nobody said it would be easy!) Through whatever channel I could, I stayed focused on bringing good things to other women, whether it was through parenting tips, reflections on faith, business advice, or humor. Some things worked, some not, but I kept going.

I spent the next year of my life learning how to build a blog and run an online business. I never let my fear of failure stop me (and trust me, I failed as much as I succeeded!). I just plowed through any reservations I had, never feeling I had to ask anyone for permission to try new things. If I didn't know how to do something, I researched it and tried it. It's funny that I say that, because "home Alli" was such an introvert, naturally fearful, and not a big risk taker. "Internet Alli" was outgoing, fearless, and daring. My work blogging was actually helping me develop new skills and abilities. It was stretching my capacity and allowing me to do things I never imaged I would be able to do.

I think God had been developing those characteristics and abilities in me long before he ever set my feet on this path, but it was still amazing to watch those stored-away gifts begin to unfold. Each of us is called to do something great in this world.

And even if the circumstances and the timing are difficult, discovering the place where we get to do what we were created to do is a great gift.

Now, if you think this all seems very neat and tidy, I should add that the year after I started my blog was the year we had our fifth son and lost our home. During those six weeks that we lived with my grandfather in the mountains of East Tennessee, we didn't even have Internet. I used to drive to a McDonald's Playland with free Wi-Fi and let the kids play while I wrote my blog posts and answered email to the sounds of children screaming and playing in the background. Easy? Nope. Worth it? You bet it was! My passion was awakened, and I got busy building a business.

> **EACH OF US IS CALLED TO DO SOMETHING GREAT IN THIS WORLD. DISCOVERING THE PLACE WHERE WE GET TO DO WHAT WE WERE CREATED TO DO IS A GREAT GIFT.**

Busy with a Purpose

After the tears, the "God, have your way with us" prayer, and our newfound humility, we settled back in Nashville, and I focused on building a business online with the passion that only a woman who didn't want to ever move again could have. I had an old laptop with broken keys, forty dollars to spend on business books, and a determination to find a way to support our family, so if anything happened to my husband's job, we would have the backup plan we didn't have before.

I nursed my smallest guy, Jeremiah, on one knee and balanced that broken laptop on my other knee and worked my tail off every day. And as hard as that was, I realized I was no longer *striving* to find myself or my purpose. I was no longer busy doing things just to make a good impression on others or to make others happy. Instead, I was taking daily steps to build a business from the online magazine I created. I had broken the cycle of busy without purpose; I was now a woman on a mission.

I think sometimes we allow our circumstances to dictate our actions, good and bad. When I was bored and lonely and trying to be supermom, I let my feelings and my circumstances convince me I'd be happier if I just kept busy, if I just kept pleasing others. But the more I strived, and the more I focused on myself and my needs and my feelings, the more *unhappy* I became. However, when our life and financial circumstances forced me to focus on God instead of everything and everyone else (including myself), I became motivated to live my life doing what God wanted me to do.

BlissDom

Within just a few months after moving back to Nashville, I met my future conference cofounder, and we threw our very own blogging business conference. The concept of a blogging business conference was so new that we made it up as we went along. Our initial concept was for small business owners, bloggers, and writers to gather, encourage, and learn from each other. On a whim, we decided to call it BlissDom. Our first event had a hundred women in attendance, all of whom I had met through my blog. The hilarity of that event is still a great memory. We held the one-day event as a panel-style conference, full of women sharing their stories, lessons, and best practices for their websites and businesses in the bar of a local hotel. I was on the panel, wearing my newborn son in a baby wrap. It was like a scene straight out of the movie *Sweet Home Alabama*, with me wearing my baby ... in a bar.

Until the day we actually held our event, I didn't admit to Barbara, the cofounder of the BlissDom conference, that I had never actually *attended* a conference. It was easy enough for me to Google how to run a successful conference (I told you I loved discovering new things!), get tips, ask my friends who had been to them what speakers they liked, and then follow best practices. I guess bringing my nursing baby just seemed like the natural thing to do because at no point did I realize I would actually be speaking to the group.

I gave Barbara the schedule I had prepared, and as she looked at it she said, "Okay, Alli, you left off your opening remarks to the group. Go ahead and start with that."

I said, "Oh, I missed that? Do we have to do those?"

"Yes," Barbara said incredulously.

"Oh, um, I can't. You see, um, I haven't told you this, but I'm shy and can't speak to people like that. You do it?"

Barbara laughed and said, "Alli, everyone here is a friend of yours. You invited them. Get over yourself and get up there and welcome them!"

I did it, but it's a miracle my baby-wearing self didn't faint from the terror of it.

Looking back on how BlissDom began, I see that I had no business thinking I could start and run a conference. The world would have said I wasn't good enough to do what I was doing. I didn't have the qualifications or experience. It was one of many times in my life that God plunked me down in a situation and got my attention. He had plans for how to use the gifts he planted inside of me. I had to grow up and develop them a little (okay, a lot!). That took time, courage, and a willingness to do things badly (like welcoming the group in a cold sweat because I hadn't seen or Googled "opening remarks" from sample schedules I used as my template) on the way to doing them well. Or as the prophet Zechariah put it, "Do not despise these small beginnings, for the LORD rejoices to see the work begin" (Zechariah 4:10 NLT).

Over the next five years, the BlissDom conference grew faster than we ever dreamed. It was the first thing I had ever done that I felt truly successful at, beyond being a wife and mom. I served as the cofounder, chief creative officer, conference host, and I oversaw community and content. As BlissDom grew, my cofounder and I added a third partner and began to hire additional staff. Not only was BlissDom successful as a conference, it also built great business networks for me and for many on the BlissDom team. It provided an outlet for the attendees to fully develop their talents, build support groups, meet with big brands, and launch their own businesses. In just five short years, BlissDom became a household name in the online community and provided an incredible means of financial security for my family as well as for my partners and others. It was crazy good.

● ● ● ● ● ●

GOD PLANTS GIFTS IN US AND PROVIDES OPPORTUNITIES THROUGHOUT OUR LIVES TO FULFILL OUR LIFE'S PURPOSE.

We went international and held an annual event in Toronto, which was later franchised, as well as in Nashville. We sold out, had corporate sponsors that gave us big budgets, hosted celebrity guests, and even had private concerts with Matt Kearney, Harry Connick Jr. (whom I had secretly had a major crush on since I was a freshman in high school), and the country band Rascal Flatts.

My grandfather used to say, "Find something you love doing, and you'll never work a day in your life." Miraculously, I found something I was passionate about that flowed out of the gifts God had given me.

My greatest joy with BlissDom was getting to bring in so many different people, speakers, and communities. Every year hundreds of people told me that initially they were afraid to come because so many of the attendees were of the Christian faith. They were afraid the Christians would be cliquish, judgmental, or forceful in trying to convert them to Christianity. But afterward many would share how great the experience had been. I realized then that BlissDom was something special. It was a place where large numbers of Christians and non-Christians got together and had a party. To me it was beautiful, and I knew without a doubt I had found my calling forever.

Little did I know, God would give me many different ways to work out my calling, and they wouldn't all involve BlissDom.

Fearfully and Wonderfully Made

That whisper in my spirit years ago to write a book led me on the journey to start blogging, and that led me to BlissDom, and that led to me writing this to you now. The journey was bumpy, sometimes easy, sometimes scary, but always a predestined trip.

I have learned that God plants gifts in us and provides opportunities throughout our lives to fulfill our life's purpose. But we have to break the cycle of busy in our lives if we are going to have enough room to discover God's plan — our destiny.

Let the implications of that sink in for a minute. The Creator of the universe has a plan for your life. The very God who spoke the world into motion, created you for a purpose.

Psalm 139 says,

> **WE HAVE TO BREAK THE CYCLE OF BUSY IN OUR LIVES IF WE ARE GOING TO HAVE ENOUGH ROOM TO DISCOVER OUR DESTINY.**

For you created my inmost being;
    you knit me together in my mother's womb.
I praise you because I am fearfully and wonderfully made;

> your works are wonderful,
> I know that full well.
> My frame was not hidden from you
>   when I was made in the secret place,
>   when I was woven together in the depths of the earth.
> Your eyes saw my unformed body;
>   all the days ordained for me were written in your book
>   before one of them came to be. (Psalm 139:13–16)

He created us, you and me, with a beginning — a beautiful, handcrafted, laden-with-purpose beginning. And he has ordained an ending for us: "All the days ordained for me were written in your book before one of them came to be."

God has set our feet on a path that leads to where and how we can live out our calling. We often make ourselves very busy because we are searching for our calling. But it is when we slow down and choose to be busy only when what we are doing is our God-given purpose that we can see where God is leading us.

I want it to comfort you that you do not have to strive endlessly to be good enough or to work hard enough to find God's plan for you. If you stay focused on God, you will not miss your destiny.

Marbles in a Jar

A while back I was talking with a friend, trying to help her understand how the passions of her life held the key to the mystery of her purpose. But I just couldn't make the point well enough, so I told her this story:

When I was a little girl, one of my favorite things to do with my mom was to go to flea markets. I loved digging through piles of junk to find a treasure that no one else appreciated.

One day I found a lamp made from a mason jar half-filled with marbles. I loved that lamp from the moment I saw it. I took it home, cleaned it up, and proudly set it on my nightstand. I used my flashlight to shine a bright light through the jar. The light reflected off the marbles in different ways, creating a pretty pattern on the wall of my bedroom.

Later I opened the jar and found my favorite marbles. Some of the marbles were clear, some multicolored, some heavier weighted, and some even made of metal. For the fun of it, I took out the duds, the marbles I didn't like, then sent light through the marbles again. This time the light patterns were sharper, more brilliant. Then I rearranged the marbles that were left, creating a pattern that was even prettier. Using the light, I kept experimenting, moving marbles around, removing and adding to create the perfect kaleidoscope of color on the wall.

I told my friend that day, "We are like that mason jar, filled with amazing, unique gifts, things we are passionate about and love doing. But our jar is often filled with some 'duds' as well, perhaps expectations that were piled onto us, or things or activities we thought we should keep that are just keeping us busy without a purpose."

As we start breaking busy in our lives, tossing out the duds and moving around what's left, our gifts and passions will shine with brighter brilliance. As we discover our

• • • • • •

AS WE START BREAKING BUSY IN OUR LIVES, OUR PURPOSE BEGINS TO SHINE BRIGHTLY AND CLEARLY.

passions and allow God to craft them into beautiful patterns, we begin to see what we are called to do on this earth, and our purpose begins to shine forth with color and clarity.

God buried treasure inside each of us. Our gifts, our strengths, our passions. What we do with the gifts is up to us. Like a gardener who must faithfully tend, weed, and water her plot of ground, we have to diligently nurture the gifts planted in us.

Jesus told a parable that makes this point so brilliantly.

> A man going on a journey ... called his servants and entrusted his wealth to them. To one he gave five bags of gold, to another two bags, and to another one bag, each according to his ability. Then he went on his journey. The man who received five bags of gold went at once and put his money to work and gained five bags more. So also, the one with two bags of gold gained two more. But the man who had received one bag went off, dug a hole in the ground and hid his master's money. (Matthew 25:14–18)

The story goes on to say that when the man returned and realized that both the first and second servants had used their master's wealth wisely, he praised them saying, "Well done, good and faithful servant! You have been faithful with a few things; I will put you in charge of many things" (vv. 21, 23). But what of the servant who had placed his master's wealth in a hole in the ground? Naturally, the master was not pleased, and the man with one unused talent was cast outside into the darkness.

God has entrusted each of us with great gifts — namely our time, talents, and treasures — and he calls us to manage them well, whether they be many or few.

I don't know about you, but I definitely want to be the servant who hears, "Well done, good and faithful servant."

How to Identify and Fuel Your Passions

In his book *The Purpose Driven Life*, Rick Warren writes,

> The search for the purpose of life has puzzled people for thousands of years. That's because we typically begin at the

wrong starting point — ourselves. We ask self-centered questions like, What do I want to be? What should I do with my life? What are my goals, my ambitions, my dreams for my future? But focusing on ourselves will never reveal our life's purpose.[8]

It's so easy to get caught up in our plans for our life and completely miss the point. As Warren points out in a chapter titled "It All Starts with God." Or as Solomon wrote: "Many are the plans in a person's heart, but it is the LORD's purpose that prevails" (Proverbs 19:21). If you want to know your life's purpose, you have to begin with the Creator of your life and ask *him* what he wants you to do.

I had a lot of plans. Where we would live, what kind of house we would own, how many kids we would have. It took God breaking me to break my busy, striving ways and teach me to seek him. Once I started truly seeking God (not seeking him *for* something, but seeking his face, spending time with him, building a relationship with him), I began to notice patterns in my life, my "marbles in the jar." I began to realize that God had given me a passion for certain things. I also noticed that while my passions didn't change over time, the way they played out did, and that was okay. As long as I was seeking God and using the gifts he had given me, he would direct how and where he wanted me to use them.

Sometimes, though, identifying our passions and using them in the best possible way can be difficult. We want to be good stewards of our gifts, like the first two servants in the story in Matthew, but sometimes we just cannot see what our gifts are (even when we are connected to God). It's okay to admit that we don't always know the answers.

Here are some questions you can ask yourself as you go through the process of identifying and placing your passions in their optimal setting.

1. What activities have you loved since childhood?

People always told me as a little girl that I had an inexhaustible desire to learn and tell everyone who would listen what I had discovered — to the point where I actually exhausted their ability to want to listen. I was the kid who read encyclopedias!

Bringing good information to people is still my passion, and I'm still learning every single day. Only now, instead of being the girl who corners her poor friends saying, "Let me tell you what I just discovered," I'm doing it here, online, and on TV.

Like me, my friend Jean just loved to read as a kid and visited the library weekly (though her library's limit was a mere six books!). Her love of books took her on a journey from working in a local library as a college student, to interning and working for a publishing company, to writing her own books. Clear communication that glorifies God became her passion, and reading is still one of her favorite things to do. In fact, after she reads all day for work, what does she do in the evening? You guessed it. She reads!

2. Discover what you love

If not for dipping my toes into the online world, I never in a million years would have discovered I liked hosting events. I saw myself as a shy introvert who was terrified of large social situations.

But the process of sharing my life online, making new friendships through conferences, and embracing new challenges and business opportunities changed me.

I tried new things like public speaking and business consulting, things far outside my comfort zone. Some things worked, some things did not, but along the journey I got clear on what my passions and my callings are. Finding your calling is always a process and always involves lots of experimentation.

My friend Monica started off as a kindergarten teacher and realized quickly that she loved teaching but missed interaction with adults. So she went to work for a marketing firm, but she found long days in meetings just weren't her thing either. Frustrated with herself and her indecision (and the good number of pounds she had put on because of it), she joined a gym. Her physical transformation and the emotional one that came from taking care of herself caused her friends to start asking what she was doing. She loved motivating others toward good health. Once she became a personal trainer, she realized she was still teaching (her true passion), she was motivating others (born to be an encourager), and she believed she was making a difference in the lives of others. She just needed to experiment a bit to discover her purpose.

3. What tugs at your heart?

What organization tugs at you to join, what problem cries out that you would love to fix, or what ways would you love to help? For me, as soon as I started blogging and getting to know others online, I wanted to help build others up. I wanted to help women see their God-given potential and abilities. Sometimes I did that by bringing in a certain speaker at an event. Sometimes I wrote articles that shared recommendations for products or books. Whatever it was that I found helpful, I couldn't wait to share.

My friend Tami found that her heart broke for the kids in the orphanage that our church supported in Haiti. She and her husband supported the orphanage and visited as often as their schedules allowed. Even though they were grandparents, God tugged on their hearts to adopt one of the girls they were so passionate about serving. Tami and her husband now have their daughter home, and they celebrate every day together. Her heart's calling gave Tami a clue to her next life mission.

4. If money were no object, what would you do for free?

I often joke that if we won the lottery, never had to work again, and bought our own tropical island, I would still be logging in to some livestream and yelling at people, "Do you know what opportunities you have at your fingertips? Go! Find your God-given destiny!"

For me, the experience of teaching myself how to build a business online showed me that anyone can do it. The desperate situation my family was in at that time fueled me to keep going, even though my fears told me that I didn't know what I was doing (which was kind of true), I wasn't good enough, and I was wasting my time.

So from that imaginary island that I'll buy if we win the lottery, I'll forever tell anyone who will listen that we live in an age of endless opportunities, and we don't need permission to try them.

All you need is the willingness to uncover and invest in the gifts that God has given you.

A good friend shared with me the story about a lady who loves to sew and often dreamed about turning her passion into a business. But anytime she started a new business, it was a failure. Finally she realized that although she loved sewing, she didn't love the stress of being a business owner (which, hey, is totally legit if you've ever owned your own business). So she started sewing and donating isolette covers for the newborns in the neonatal intensive care unit in hospitals, a gift that blessed the families in distress there. Many families now have one of her gifts in their nursery at home.

5. What energizes you?

Look around at everything you do — marriage, parenting, work, volunteering, being a great neighbor. As you look, ask yourself, *What energizes me?*

Jennifer, a woman I met at a conference, once told me the only thing she was good at was bossing people around. She said, "I'm not just good at it, it energizes me. It makes me come to life." Once a driven business executive turned stay-at-home mom, turned empty nester, she was bored and floundering a bit with her new stage of life. I asked her if she had ever thought about becoming a small business consultant, since she had the credentials for it. She emailed me several months later and told me she'd taken my advice and was "killing it" as a consultant.

6. What is something everyone says you are good at?

Sometimes you can't see your own gifts, but everyone else can. My girlfriend Lori believed she had nothing to offer to the world. Despite the fact that all her friends told her what a great listener she was and how wise her advice was, she never felt as if she had a marketable talent. At age fifty-three, however, she determined to pursue something she felt good about. So she studied and became a certified life coach, a job she finds incredibly fulfilling.

Lori was stunned to realize her friends had been right all along. Isn't that so often the case in our lives? I know I have a tendency to not give as much weight to the opinions of people who know me best. But if a stranger affirms the same thing my closest friends tell me, *then* I believe it. We are all sometimes predictably silly humans!

A Lifetime of Passion and Gifts

Now keep in mind these questions are not just about finding your career. In my case, my passions became my career, but we are not limited to that. Our passions and gifts are about us as whole people, not just what we do for a living!

I have a friend whose passion is helping women and children in need. Her vocation is writing, and while she loves to write, it is not her purpose on this earth. She writes so she can afford to help women and children in need, her true passion.

So if you don't have a job, don't think you need to find one to use your gifts and fulfill your purpose. God uses us at *all* our life stages, developing gifts within us that we never even knew were buried inside. Embracing our passions and discovering new gifts throughout our life, whether in our twenties or in our nineties, is the beauty of a life lived inside the will of God.

As we mature and go through life, we discover the "big things" (career, achievements) often aren't as important as the "little things," using the gifts God planted in us in a variety of circumstances — in our careers, yes, but also in volunteer work, family, and church involvement.

Psalm 92:12–15 says,

The righteous will flourish like a palm tree,
    they will grow like a cedar of Lebanon;
planted in the house of the LORD,
    they will flourish in the courts of our God.
They will still bear fruit in old age,
    they will stay fresh and green,
proclaiming, "The LORD is upright;
    he is my Rock, and there is no wickedness in him."

What a beautiful description of a life lived fully and faithfully using the gifts God gives us.

Finding your passions that lead to your purpose may feel difficult at times, but remember this: God's not keeping it a secret from you. He's waiting for you to stop striving and set everything aside that is keeping you busy and distracted, then turn your attention to him. In a living, daily relationship, he can then show you places you should go, people you should listen to, talents you should nourish, opportunities you should pursue, and passions and gifts he wants you to develop.

Whatever your age or season of life, new adventures are waiting for you. Walking in your God-given destiny is the best kind of life you can possibly live. True, your life may still be busy. But instead of breaking you, your busyness will bless you, and it will bless the world God sent you to serve. And in a world full of senseless striving, you will have the joy of living out your God-given, unique, and wonderful purpose.

Action Steps

1. Go back and answer the six questions in this chapter. What insights come forth?

2. Identify a passion you would like to pursue or a gift you would like to develop, praying to God for his guidance.

3. Plan to take one step in pursuing that passion or gift. You'll be tempted to plan it all and get overwhelmed, but don't. Just take the first step and be faithful on the journey God takes you on.

FOUR

EDITING

Finding God's Best in a World of Options

In the spring of 2012, I was at a large church leadership conference in Orange County, California, loving the worship and messages and (as always) keeping an eye out for potential speakers for my BlissDom event. During the prayer time, as I prayed about the theme for next year's conference, I very clearly felt God nudge me with two words, "Quit BlissDom."

Surely I didn't hear that right. "Quit BlissDom?" Why in the world would God tell me to quit BlissDom? The very thought of quitting the company I had built over the previous five years was like hearing that I needed to chop off my own foot or give up chocolate. Tears stung my eyes as I sat there in complete disbelief.

The great thing about a Christian conference is that you can cry in public and everyone will just assume you are super spiritual and having a "God moment," which I guess in hindsight I *was* having. But my God moment wasn't all warm and fuzzy.

The God of the universe had just spoken to me. Not audibly, mind you, but he may as well have. I've learned through the years that when I am both surprised and challenged by a whisper in my spirit, it's God asking me to do something that stretches my limited concept of what I can do.

God's message that April afternoon wasn't some affectionate encouragement, telling me I was on the right track or that he loved me. It was: "Quit that thing you've built. That thing that succeeded beyond your wildest dreams. That thing that has provided for your family — that is *still* providing for your family." My God moment had me itching to jump out of my seat and make a mad dash for the nearest exit.

After about fifteen minutes I looked up and saw my friend Tami sitting down the row from me. Noticing the expression on my face, she said, "Alli, what is wrong?"

I blurted out, "Tami, I was praying about work, and God told me to quit BlissDom. Can you believe that?"

Tami is one of my mentors. She is wise and thoughtful and loves Jesus. She looked back at me calmly and smiled. Then she said the strangest thing. "Well, Alli, that can't be all that much of a surprise with how God has been working in your life lately. How do you feel about it?"

How did I feel about it? How did I *feel* about it? Well, now, wasn't that the question of the day! I, being the spiritual giant that I am, fought back tears and said, oh so eloquently, "How do I feel about it? I feel like crap. That's how I feel about it. I guess I'll walk away from my company and what I love. And one day I'll tell this story, and I'll sound very holy, and it will all sound very spiritual, but for now I feel like crap."

Did I Really Hear That?

Leaving the conference, I pulled myself together and somehow made it to the door. Of course, I had to run into several people I knew before I could make my exit, one of whom was my good friend Lindsey. She handed me a new book written by one of our mutual friends, Jennie, and as we made small talk, I casually tossed the book into my bag. Honestly, at that point everything was a blur. I needed to be alone, alone with my thoughts and my millions of unanswered questions.

I'd love to tell you that I took Tami's words and joyfully made the decision to obey God right then and there. I would sound really spiritual then, right? But that isn't truth, and it isn't the way most of us come to terms with tough choices we have to make in our lives. I was appalled at the thought of leaving. Appalled. Leaving was not an option I had ever even considered.

That night in my bed at the hotel, I stared at the ceiling and wrestled with questions like, *Did I really hear that? If I did* [and I really knew I did, I was just trying to stall], *can I trust God that he is doing something in my life that I can't see yet even though it all seems terrible right now? Am I going crazy?*

GOD SOMETIMES CALLS US TO QUIT THINGS THAT ARE GOOD IN EXCHANGE FOR HIS PLANS THAT ARE GREATER.

On the flight home, I asked God for two signs because, in my present state of emotions, one sign wasn't going to be enough. It was just too crazy to trust that a small, inaudible voice inside me said to walk away from the company and the community I had built. What if I heard it wrong? I really, really wanted to be wrong. So I began looking for proof that I was, in fact, wrong.

As I settled into my flight home to Nashville, I remembered the book Lindsey gave me. I wasn't interested in reading anything, but I knew my obsessing about what I had to do wasn't healthy, so why not read and distract myself?

And as I read Jennie Allen's book *Anything*, it was as though she had written the whole book for me to read on that plane and to tell me to *do it*.

> Stepping out wholly dependent on God to come through, stepping away from what is secure and comfortable, exposes holes in our faith. Something about stepping off cliffs where God leads allows God the opportunity to move in greater ways. When we step off and he shows up, we see him differently than we would if we were standing safely looking over the edge.[9]

All right, God. I get it. This is my first sign. You want me to leap into the unknown. Great.

Sigh.

Submissive ... Sort Of

On the drive home from the airport, I told God that the next sign was all about my husband. I planned to tell him the news after the kids went to school the next morning and let him decide what we should do. I mean, wasn't that biblical? Truth be told, I was trying to outsmart God (I wish I was kidding). I thought I had my out by being submissive to Mark. There was no way a man with an MBA, Mr. All-About-the-Bottom-Line, was going to let me quit BlissDom.

Mark had just retired from the great job that had allowed us to move back to Nashville a few years before. As I was building and running BlissDom, Mark and I had both worked full-time at incredibly demanding jobs, Mark at the hospital and me at home, but we had come to see that the kids needed one of us to focus on them. So Mark, following a clear calling of God to "raise our boys" and manage our family, left his job. (It wasn't just me who God was telling to quit things!)

I was the sole breadwinner in our family now, so the idea of my telling him, "Hey, honey, God told me to quit and I have no idea what is next," and Mark to reply, "Great. Who needs a stable income? Let's do this!" was laughable.

Here's how the conversation with my husband actually went. (Imagine us sitting on the couch in the living room.)

"So, Mark, I'm pretty sure God told me to quit BlissDom and walk away from everything," I blurted.

"Are you sure?"

"Yes, I'm sure." (I told him the whole story of asking for a sign and reading Jennie's book.)

"Just Canada?" (BlissDom had two annual large events, one in the US and one franchised event in Canada.)

"No qualifiers. Just quit BlissDom."

"After this year?"

"No qualifiers."

Now understand that my husband is a very even-keeled guy. I call him my rock. Where I am one who cries at commercials and am prone to emotional highs and lows, he is calm and practical. So his response was beyond anything I could have predicted. He paused for a minute, we sat in an awkward silence, and then he said, "You'd better call Barbara [my BlissDom cofounder] and tell her you are quitting."

All right, God, you win.

It was official. I was quitting. Not that day, not right then. *But soon*, I promised myself (and God). *As soon as I know what to do next.*

Frozen in Fear

A month or two after I heard the message to quit, I ran into Tami again. When she asked me how I was doing, I all but burst into tears. I leaned in close and whispered, "I still don't know what I'm supposed to do. I know I'm supposed to quit, but God won't tell me what is next. I'm doing what is in front of me right now, but I don't really know what I'm supposed to do." In short, I was a mess.

I looked good to the outside world, to my friends at church, and on Instagram and Facebook (isn't that how we do it?), but inside I was terrified. I was having a slow-motion nervous breakdown with a smile on my face.

It would've been great if God sent me a memo saying, "Walk away from this. It will be humbling. You'll have to clear out some sin in your life. You are too prideful, too big for your britches, and you've once again forgotten to rely on me in your daily life. You'll struggle temporarily to find the next right path, and in the meantime I'll be growing and maturing you. But don't worry, it will all work out perfectly according to my plan."

But that memo never came.

And believe me, I waited for it.

I was frozen in fear, terrified I'd lose friends, terrified I'd lose important business connections, terrified I'd fail financially, and terrified people would view me as some crazy religious fanatic. Between my fear and my pride, I could not do what I knew God was telling me to do. How was I going to tell these people who had built this business alongside me that the God of the universe had spoken to me and told me simply, "Quit BlissDom"?

It wasn't going to make sense to them. There's something about the words "God told me to" that can make nonbelievers worry you're hearing voices and even some believers say, "What? You're playing the God card?"

In my heart, I knew I had only one *real* option — to obey God — but in my mind, I tried to create several options that let me have an out so I wouldn't seem like a kook to my friends and coworkers. Four months later, my best friend, Megan, said to me, "Alli, if God told you to leave but you are staying, no matter how noble you think your reasons, you are cheating on Jesus." She went on to say, "I know that you are afraid and too proud to just walk away, but I know that when you leave, you aren't going to fail — you are going to fly."

I believed I had heard God accurately. I believed he loved me and had great plans for my future. But despite my belief and my trust in him, it took me a little more than a year to obey — a long, miserable, grueling year of indecision and disobedience.

From Good to Great

My eventual announcement to the company that it was time for me to walk away from BlissDom definitely freaked everyone out. I'm pretty sure they decided to wait until "Alli was out of her Jesus phase" and hoped I would change my mind. But that change of mind never came.

My decision impacted others financially and professionally. Members of the BlissDom community, upon hearing the news that the annual BlissDom conference was ending, were heartbroken. Tweets, Facebook updates, and Instagram posts of disappointment and sadness rolled in for days. Even though I was walking away in obedience, doing what I was called to do, I still felt terrible about disappointing others in the process. Sometimes doing what is right still feels like a punch in the gut.

• • • • • •
GOD SOMETIMES CALLS US TO EDIT OUT SOMETHING GOOD IN OUR LIVES TO MAKE ROOM FOR SOMETHING GREAT.

Maybe life has been that way for you. You've come to a cross-roads, and it's time to make a choice. You know you need to prune some branches that are fruitful to make room for a bigger harvest to come. But in doing that, you may disappoint others or even cause them pain. It's not easy, and it would be dishonest for me to tell you this story while leaving out the moments when I broke down in tears and cried out to God, asking why.

Here's the thing about breaking busy. Sometimes it calls for tough choices, for making drastic changes even in the places where you've been highly successful. I call these kinds of choices "edits."

Webster defines the action of editing as "to alter, adapt, or refine especially to bring about conformity to a standard or to suit a particular purpose."[10]

God was trying to alter my life and was refining my character to suit his particular purpose. But sometimes edits hurt, and sometimes they cause others to hurt. When you feel the need to edit something out of your life, expecting the process to be easy will only make that change harder. Like most growth in life, editing out the good is not easy, but it is ultimately worth it.

As the days went by, I realized I wanted God to rescue me from the pain I was in and the pain I was causing. I was saying, "Okay, God, I'm obeying you. Now give me the rundown. Show me the plan." But his plan wasn't to rescue me. It was to teach me things I needed to learn. I needed to trust that God would use my decision, prompted by him, in others' lives as well.

When God told me to quit BlissDom, he was asking me to not lean on my own understanding. I had to rely on him, to focus on the Word, to pray, and to seek wise counsel. I had stepped out into the unknown, trusting that God would somehow, some-time, somewhere show up.

We Get to Choose

Every fruitful life goes through a process of editing, where some parts of our lives are carved out, trimmed away, or rearranged to make room for better ones. Sometimes we initiate the editing. Other times, God steps in more directly to command us to edit.

What I learned in the year it took me to walk away was that when God told me to leave, he also gave me the option to choose what to do. I could have ignored him and denied I heard that still, small voice. I could have kept going in my busy world and pushed the call to leave from my mind. Or I could choose to trust him.

It reminds me of a favorite quote from Steven Furtick:

There's always a tradeoff. Before God can bring his promises to pass in your life, he has to strip away all the stuff that keeps you from trusting him wholeheartedly. And that stuff is on the inside. God's invisible work in you prepares you for his visible works through you.[11]

God knew that there were areas in my life that were unhealthy, places I needed to heal, and my wishy-washy faith needed to grow strong. How would that happen? Probably not through continued success in all the ways the world measures success, but through stepping away from the easy and stepping into the unknown, where he was calling me to trust his plans for me.

"For my thoughts are not your thoughts,
    neither are your ways my ways,"
      declares the Lord.
"As the heavens are higher than the earth,
    so are my ways higher than your ways
    and my thoughts than your thoughts." (Isaiah 55:8–9)

We don't always have to know what God's plans are for us, only that they are better than we could ever dream and always for the best. When he brings us to a fork in the road, we won't know what lies beyond the choice of obedience or disobedience, but we do know that his ways are better and wiser than ours.

God's Guardrails

Sometimes edits are all about what we need to stop doing if we are to live the life God created us to live. I call those "proactive edits." Leaving BlissDom was a proactive edit (more on that later).

The other type of edit is a "natural edit." Natural edits are the limitations we all have and the losses we all suffer. A natural edit is an edit we don't make for ourselves, but that is with us from birth or is made in the course of living our lives. It can be something simple, or it can be a dramatic change in the scenery of our lives, a course correction or guardrail we come upon suddenly that guides us back to the path God has for us.

Let me tell you about a natural edit in my own life.

Have you ever watched shows like *The Voice* or *American Idol* and thought, "Goodness gracious, did these people's families not love them enough to tell them they can't sing?"

Sadly, I was one of those kids. I used to sing my heart out, and my mom always encouraged me and praised my singing ability. It wasn't until third grade, when a friend and I were riding in the backseat of my car and my friend announced that I was a terrible singer that I realized I couldn't sing at all. All I thought about in that moment of humiliation was, *Why has Mom been telling me I am a great singer all my life?* In addition to being devastated about not being able to sing, I was miffed at my mom for never giving me a heads-up!

Now, in my mom's defense, she believed she was helping to boost my self-esteem. This was right in the middle of the self-esteem movement, when parenting experts taught parents to teach their kids that they were awesome and perfect. And Mom probably really did love my singing, because that's how moms are. I sing, however, like two rabid cats fighting in an alley under a full moon.

Still, if it were up to me, I would be a singer. I would sing all day long, I would fill up stadiums, go on the Grand Ole Opry and headline tours, and wear fabulous outfits. But that's obviously not God's plan for my life. No matter what I do, no matter how much I want it, it's not going to happen.

My lack of singing ability, that which makes dogs howl and babies cry, is a natural edit. And though I was spoon-fed sayings like, "The world is your oyster" and "You can do anything you set your mind to," this is simply not the truth. We want to believe that we have all the options of the world available to us and that we can overcome limitations if we just try hard enough.

The reality is, we didn't choose where or to whom we were born. We didn't choose what we would look like or what our talents or passions would be. It can be frustrating to realize that we don't have as much control over our lives as we once thought.

In other words, natural edits can be painful. Friends drop us. We get a job, but not the job we wanted. A health challenge limits our capacity. Finances limit our college options. We don't have the energy to be both full-time employee and classroom mother for our children's classes. Divorce, job loss, and other devastations upend our lives, and how we respond to those natural edits defines our future.

When we stay stuck in our losses and focused on how life is different than what we wanted it to be, we miss what God has for us. But when we learn to look at our limitations as helpful guidance, we see how beneficial they are to our life. They keep us focused on where we are going and keep us from straying off into areas where we don't belong. They also help us see what gifts and choices we *do* have. Because working in the background of our lives is an architect, a God about whom it is written:

> My frame was not hidden from you
>> when I was made in the secret place,
>> when I was woven together in the depths of the earth.
> Your eyes saw my unformed body;
>> all the days ordained for me were written in your book
>> before one of them came to be. (Psalm 139:15–16)

God's plan is *always* better than the one we have in mind! I've prayed for God to bless certain dreams of mine, to make a certain boy love me back, to give me the talent to reach a certain goal, to help me get to a certain career goal, and to all these things he lovingly, silently said no. He loves me enough not to grant me all the desires of my heart because his plan is better. And he does the same thing for you. His no always prepares us for his perfect yes.

God has set our feet upon a path that he created for us, a path that leads us to our calling, our purpose for being on this earth. When we try to design our own path, taking advantage of every opportunity that comes along without thought to how God designed us, we end up overwhelmed, feeling like failures — and way too busy.

● ● ● ● ● ●

GOD'S NO ALWAYS PREPARES US FOR HIS PERFECT YES.

But mercifully, God, in his wisdom, edits. He sets guardrails along the path — natural edits — to keep us focused, dependent on him, and moving in the right direction toward the life we were created to live.

What Did Jesus Do?

In that year that I was working up my courage and faith to finally walk away from BlissDom, I stayed busy distracting myself with ideas for new companies to start, hobbies to pick up, and projects to take on. What I needed was to accept that God was putting on the brakes to get me to focus on him and learn to trust his plans, not mine. My calling *at that time* was to obey, to quit my busyness and my business, and do nothing else except wait.

Sometimes our calling requires us to pass up lots of great opportunities because, no matter how great it is, if it's not what we are supposed to be doing, it won't produce fruit.

Jesus was both busy *and* fruitful in his time on earth. He healed the blind, the sick, the paralyzed, and even raised people from the dead. We, on the other hand, are just busy with our busyness. I know Jesus was given plenty of opportunities to do more, but he didn't say yes to everything because he wasn't called to do everything. Luke 4:42–43 says,

> At daybreak, Jesus went out to a solitary place. The people were looking for him and when they came to where he was, they tried to keep him from leaving them. But he said, "I must proclaim the good news of the kingdom of God to the other towns also, because that is why I was sent."

If Jesus himself, Lord of the universe yet bound in a human body, didn't do more than God called him to do, neither should we. Jesus accepted his natural limitations (a human body born in ancient Israel), then lived a life of proactive edits, actively choosing each day to follow God's calling for his life. We too must accept our limitations, then begin proactively editing our lives as we seek to live out our calling.

How to Make Proactive Edits

Here are some practical ways you can make edits in your life and break busy before busy breaks you (and it will, trust me!).

1. Be proactive, not reactive

A proactive edit is one we make in advance, before things get out of control. A reactive edit is one we make once a crisis hits. It's a reaction to something gone wrong (typically) and *most reactive edits are not good ones.*

Here's what I mean. A proactive edit, an edit that you make on purpose, can be as simple as saying no to baking cookies or coaching a team, or as challenging as saying no to extra work or even a promotion at work to make way for spending precious time with your family.

A reactive edit comes about most often due to an overcommitted schedule. Perhaps you say yes to too many people, only to realize you aren't going to be able to fulfill your obligations. Then, in a panicked meltdown moment (come on, you know you've had one), you reactively declare, "That's it. I'm NOT baking those cookies tonight. They can just make do with what they have." Or maybe you do take that new promotion at work even though you know it's going to rob you of time with your family, and then several weeks or months down the road, you realize your relationship with your family is suffering tremendously, and you have to quit your job.

So why do we tend to err on the side of reactive edits instead of proactive ones? Because often proactive edits require us to let others down. We have to look people in the eye when we tell them no. We have to see the disappointment on their faces. I knew when I left BlissDom that I would let people down, and I did. In order to follow God's calling to leave BlissDom, the people pleaser in me had to die. And let me tell you, that death was a painful one. For weeks I saw people's posts on social media about how devastated they were that BlissDom was ending. For months after it was officially over, I received emails from friends telling me how disappointed they were that I could just "walk away." But in the end, I knew that if I didn't proactively edit BlissDom out of my life in obedience to God, then down the road, I would be reactively editing it. Had I held on, continuing BlissDom for many more years as my friends wanted, I would have ended up resenting them, giving BlissDom a halfhearted effort at best, and quitting in a much less positive way.

2. Discover what needs editing

Let me ask you this: What are you doing in your life right now that you would secretly be relieved to stop doing? (Now I'm not talking about walking your dog or playing board games with the kids. We all feel like not doing those things some days!) If an answer popped in your head right away (and there usually is one), then that's a good place to start when it comes to editing. I'm not saying quit everything you're doing that you don't enjoy (unless God tells you to), but for most of us, we don't have to think too hard to discover what we need to edit out of our lives.

3. Look for areas in your life that are not fruitful

Are there things in your life that you are doing, things you enjoy doing, things you're good at, but you look around and don't see a single piece of evidence you should be doing those things?

I knew a woman once who was great at storytelling. I mean, a world-class storyteller. She could make the hardest concepts seem easy because of her ability to tell a story. She loved storytelling. Loved it. So no one was surprised when she volunteered to be a storyteller in kids' church. Thing is, even though she loved it and had the skills to do it, she just didn't relate to kids well. Anytime she was the storyteller, the kids were restless, inattentive, and, honestly, kind of bored. But Maria wouldn't quit because she just *knew* she was made to be a storyteller. Finally, she took a step back and realized that God had not called her to work in kids' church. She saw a need, knew she had the raw talent, and walked through a door that wasn't really open to her. Later, Maria found her fit as a writer of stories.

Maybe in your life you've wanted to go through doors but found them closed, or, like Maria, you went through doors and realized what you were doing was unfruitful. Identifying the areas in your life that aren't producing fruit is a great way to break busy and make some proactive edits in your life. Because what you say no to determines what you say yes to.

4. Look at where God might be calling you

As my BlissDom story demonstrates, proactive edits don't just involve the deadwood. Sometimes, in fact, they seem to cut at the very heart of who we are and what (up till then) we've felt called to do. In those cases, we need to prayerfully seek God's will in our lives.

Jesus went through this process in a dramatic way at the garden of Gethsemane. His calling to preach and teach and heal was coming to a close, and God was leading him into a new and greater calling: to suffer, sacrifice his life, and be our Savior. Did Jesus shift his focus? No! He wept and struggled and prayed about this new calling in his life. Just as I had to do when God called me to leave BlissDom. (I feel in great company knowing that Jesus struggled with his new calling. He was just way better at obeying!)

5. Examine what may be hindering you

My friend Rachel is a runner. I always thought it was funny that she said she "ran for pleasure," because for the life of me, I cannot picture myself running anywhere except out of a burning building.

She told me the story of running in her first half-marathon. According to her, there is a rule in running called "nothing new on race day." It means exactly what it says. Don't buy new shoes, new socks, new sports bras ... nothing new. If you wear old things, everything will be broken in and won't rub you wrong when you're in the race.

But when Rachel arrived at her race, she realized she had left behind her utility belt, the gadget that held her water and fuel bars. She was forced to go to the runner's expo and buy a new one, meaning she would be running with a new utility belt on her very first half-marathon. Luckily, she found a top-of-the-line belt she'd had her eye on for a while, and it was on sale! She took it as a good sign.

All decked out in her running gear, including her custom-fit shoes and new utility belt, Rachel set out on her 13.1-mile route. In the beginning, all went well. The belt felt a bit looser than she liked but generally served its purpose. She was running at a pace that would likely be a personal best, and mentally she was doing well — until about mile 8. The new belt (that was a little bit loose) had been rubbing a small spot just above her hipbone, and she suddenly became aware of the pain of it.

At first it was just a small nagging pain. She kept rearranging the belt, moving it off the sore spot, but it kept moving back down to where it rubbed and chafed. By mile 10, the belt was absolutely killing her, but there was no way she could run without water and fuel, so she had to endure.

Inevitably the movement of the belt and the pain became both a mental and physical distraction. Her pace got slower and she even considered quitting. Every tenth of a mile that she passed was just a reminder of how far she still had to go. Her spectacular on-sale, top-of-the-line utility belt had become one giant hindrance.

Finally she decided, if she was going to end up quitting anyway, she may as well see if she could reach her goal without the belt and the water and fuel it held. After all, she had only 2.5 more miles to go. It took her another half mile to convince herself it was the best thing to do, but finally she reached down, unhooked the belt, and cast it off into the bushes along the course.

Getting rid of the belt gave her a huge boost mentally and physically. Spurred on by this new energy, she easily finished off those last two miles and crossed the finished line, hot, thirsty, and exhausted, but she reached her goal.

I think Rachel's story is such a great picture of this verse in Hebrews:

> Therefore, since we are surrounded by such a great cloud of witnesses, let us throw off everything that hinders and the sin that so easily entangles. And let us run with perseverance the race marked out for us. (Hebrews 12:1)

There she was, in a race she had trained for. Crowds were cheering. She was on the fast track. But then something that seemed so right at first became a hindrance. She doubted her ability to reach her goal without it, despite the fact that it was hurting her. Finally, unable to go on, she threw off the belt and finished the race.

Although it took her a while, Rachel made a proactive edit. She chose to stop doing something that was hindering her before the choice was made *for* her — in this case, having to stop running because of the pain. Identifying the hindrances in our lives is not always as easy as recognizing the troublesome belt in Rachel's running story. Sometimes we are completely unaware that we are being hindered from our goal because hindrances can come in many shapes and sizes.

How in the world can we be unaware of a hindrance? Surely if something is keeping us from reaching a goal, we'd be aware of it, right? In many cases that's correct. If our shoe is untied and we trip over it, we realize we need to stop and tie our shoe. That's an easy example of a hindrance. But what about other, less obvious hindrances? How do we identify those?

A hindrance is something that holds you back, slows you down, and keeps you from living the life you were created to live.

Sometimes hindrances can come in the form of bitterness or unforgiveness toward someone. In that case, you have to ask the Holy Spirit to help you forgive and move on from the hindrance in your heart.

Sometimes another person plays a hindering role in your life. A good friend of mine in college battled binge drinking and would go through weeks of avoiding alcohol, only to fall back into bad habits. Well, the bad-habit relapses seemed to always fall in line with when he decided to hang out with a certain group of friends. Those friends just happened to be heavy drinkers. He had to open his eyes to the fact that his friends were a hindrance to him in changing his life.

Sometimes we hinder the movement of the Holy Spirit. For me, an example of this is in my prayer life. I like to be in charge of things, and I am often certain my way is the best way to accomplish something. I've discovered that very often when I can't hear the voice of God, it's because I'm too busy telling him how I think he should accomplish things. Unfortunately, we tend to recognize hindrances only when we begin to notice bad results.

But the great news is that we can throw off those hindrances and finish the race that God has set before us.

Editing is our way to throw off our hindrances, to clear out the things that aren't part of God's perfect yes for our lives. Editing can be one of the most powerful tools to break the cycle of busyness in our lives. Finding God's yes in a world of options requires us to truly take stock of the things in our lives that have us constantly in motion. Slowing down and making prayerful decisions about what to edit out of our lives will allow us to live out our calling.

And I say *yes* to that.

Action Steps

1. What are your personal "natural edits," the limitations that you were born with or have encountered along the way?

2. Think back on a proactive edit you have taken in your life, either a small, seemingly insignificant one or a big, life-altering one. What was the good thing you had to give up in order to make room for the next great thing to happen?

3. What hindered you from taking that step?

4. What happened to you after you made that edit? In hindsight, what did you learn in that no-man's-land between "good" and the next "great"?

5. What proactive edit might God be calling you to make? How does that make you feel?

FIVE

THOUGHTS

Finding Your Peace in a World of Worry

After BlissDom closed down as an event, I waited for God to say, "Hey, Alli, good job closing BlissDom and walking away from your professional network. Here's what's next ..." But nope. Whatever was next he wasn't saying, and not only am I not good at waiting, I had bills to pay and a family to support. So I did what came naturally to me. I decided to consult and do business coaching.

After years of running BlissDom, launching and building other side projects, and consulting with large companies, becoming a consultant and a business coach was an easy next step. Helping others get unstuck, grow their businesses, or even discover what business model is right for them is easy for me. Helping large companies learn to be more human and less corporate with their communications, helping them develop productivity systems and streamline workflows, is, oddly enough, second nature for me. So when I announced I was consulting, the clients (miraculously, it seemed to me at the time) came quickly.

Within a couple of months, I had replaced my previous income from BlissDom and then some. I spent my days coaching, teaching, and consulting amazing people to success. In hindsight,

I realize what I was doing seemed like a dream life: work at home, be your own boss, work in your PJs if you wanted ... but I had never in my life been so miserable.

Even though I coached clients through getting over their fears, I was paralyzed with anxiety. As is often the case with fear and worry, there was no logical reason for me to be such a mess. I had obeyed God to leave my company. I had built a new consulting business that met our needs. Life should have felt great. But it didn't.

Walking away from the comfortable life I knew before and into the unknown felt like stepping off a cliff. And not knowing where I was going on this journey was torture. The directive to leave BlissDom had been so surprising that I felt anxious about what I would have to give up next, worried about what was coming, and terrified that I would never know. I had no control over this journey God had me on, and though I had obeyed him, I was miserable about it.

Three months after I opened my business, I started my day the usual way. My husband, Mark, shuffled the boys out the door and they were off to school like a herd of sleepy buffalo — quiet but still a force to be reckoned with.

From the big windows in my kitchen, I looked out at the green valley and hills behind our house. But despite the beauty of the sun coming up over the hills outside, I was filled with a sense of dread. I looked down at my coffee, my journal, and my notebook on the table in front of me, and I exhaled the biggest, longest, heaviest sigh.

Then I laid my forehead down on the table and began to cry. I grumbled angrily and told God how hard everything was. How I was scared and afraid.

And then he whispered to my spirit,

Get up and live like you believe that I am going to take care of you.

Oh.

Wait.

What?

Sure enough, God did what God does. In just a few words, he straightened me out and made me realize what probably was clear to anyone around me but was a revelation to me.

I was miserable because I didn't trust him. My worries were born out of my need to be in control, my desire to know what was next in my life, and a lack of gratitude for the grace he had already given me.

I had become a spoiled child grumbling that my peas were cold at the banquet he had invited me to. It's funny how Scripture pops into your head sometimes, and just as God was revealing himself to me, I thought of Psalm 23. As the Scripture came to me, so did God's reassurance:

"The LORD is my shepherd, I shall not want."

Listen to these words. I am your shepherd. You shall not live in want. I will provide for you.

"He makes me lie down in green pastures."

Look out your window.

"He leads me beside quiet waters. He restores my soul."

I have led you here to restore you, not to test you.

"He guides me in the paths of righteousness for His name's sake."

This is for my glory. Learning to let me lead you will be something you will always treasure.

"Even though I walk through the valley of the shadow of death, I fear no evil, for You are with me."

Even as you hear these words, you do not live like you believe them.

"Your rod and Your staff, they comfort me."

Believe that my boundaries and my guidance are there to be a comfort to you, to give you a sense of security.

"You prepare a table before me in the presence of my enemies."

I have placed you at a banquet table, and yet you are fearful of where your next meal will come from. Live in this moment, secure that I am with you.

"You have anointed my head with oil; My cup overflows."

I have prepared you to lead. You must only wait for me to tell you when.

"Surely goodness and lovingkindness will follow me all the days of my life, And I will dwell in the house of the LORD forever."[12]

This promise, above all else, is the one I want you to remember.

At that moment I had to decide whether I was going to keep living as if God wasn't truthful, or if I was going to live like I believed that the God of the universe, who knit me together in my mother's womb, was good and would bring me what I needed each day.

I had to learn that God was enough for me. Not my silly idea that I could do it on my own. *God* was enough for me, and I was either going to believe him to be who he said he was, or I wasn't.

At that moment I realized that life is all about our constant, ongoing choice to trust God. Instead of projecting my own frailties, wishy-washy tendencies, and weaknesses on God, I finally learned to trust that he is who he says he is.

I sat at my table staring out the window and smiled, thinking about the words of the psalmist, "He makes me lie down in green pastures" and "[he prepares] a table before me." There I was, literally sitting at a banquet table that my granddaddy gave us, looking out at green pastures. My granddaddy was a minister, and forty years ago some men in his congregation chopped down some cherry trees on his land and made the most beautiful table you've ever seen. It seats eight and weighs about a million pounds. That table sits in my eat-in kitchen in front of a wall of windows that overlook the hills that run along the back of our house.

That night as I tucked the little boys in bed, we went through our normal routine in which they shared three things they were grateful for about that day. Suddenly my newly opened eyes could see more of the problem that had made me so miserable.

There I was asking my boys to practice gratitude, but inside I was a ball of anxiety, precisely because I was ungrateful. I had become a living, walking, breathing hypocrite, busying myself with a million little things (online and off) to take my mind off my anxiety. Hours on Pinterest, hours watching Netflix, hours building and rebuilding websites because they "weren't quite perfect yet." Those were the ways I calmed my anxious heart (or tried to). Not by practicing gratitude as I was teaching my sons. No wonder I was a big messy ball of worry.

I discovered that gratitude is the antidote to anxiety.

That day I came to my senses. Finally I was able to be grateful for what God had given me, not just sad about what I left behind and annoyed that I didn't have a plan for the future and anxious about all I needed to do. I even began to anticipate what God might have for me around the corner.

Think about Such Things

My anxiety had become a destructive thought pattern that held me back from doing what God had called me to do.

Each morning, as I sat at my table consulting business owners and large corporations, I was worried about where my next customer was coming from. Each time I received a payment from a client, I worried it would be my last. And once I started down that path, I let myself spin into a full-scale meltdown over the "what ifs." What if I lost that one big client? What if I lost several small ones? What if my assistants didn't want to work with me anymore (and there was no way I could handle all this work alone)? What if we had a medical crisis or an unexpected bill? The crazy thing was we had a financial cushion. I had clients on a waiting list and knew rationally that my fears were not based in reality, but my emotions were having none of it.

My thought patterns were so destructive I had even convinced myself that I hated consulting, which simply was not true. I was so overcome with fear of the unknown that if something good happened, if I got a new big client, or a particularly positive review, or a spot on a national TV morning show (all of which happened more than once), I couldn't be grateful for it because my thoughts were all focused on negative and destructive things. You know the passage in Philippians 4:8 that says,

> Finally, brothers and sisters, whatever is true, whatever is noble, whatever is right, whatever is pure, whatever is lovely, whatever is admirable — if anything is excellent or praiseworthy — think about such things.

I was the complete and total opposite of that Scripture. Realizing that, I knew I had to make some changes in my thought patterns. So I started doing this thing that I call "truth talk." As soon as I catch myself thinking something that is negative or destructive, I stop myself by saying, "No. That isn't truth. But I know this to be true …" And then I follow that up with truth that I know from Scripture. Sometimes it is really basic

WE CAN FOCUS ON "WHATEVER IS TRUE" UNTIL TRUTH REPLACES OUR NEGATIVE THOUGHTS.

truth, like, "I know that God created man in his own image." Or "I know that God loved the world and sent his only Son that I might have everlasting life." *Jn 3:16*

will [handwritten annotation above "might"]

Whosoever believes in Him [handwritten annotation in right margin]

I keep going, focusing on "whatever is true" until truth replaces my negative thoughts and that truth takes me to a place of gratitude.

False Scripts

Even as I developed tools to break out of the anxiety cycle related to my consulting business, I had trouble breaking free of lifelong thought patterns that were more deeply entrenched in my mind.

Each of us has a false script that runs through our head, a lie we believe about God based on our life experiences. A very wise and brave mentor helped me make sense of my false script. She pointed out that I was not trusting God to provide for me and to always be there for me because my earthly father had left me at such a young age. Even though my dad did not leave me intentionally, but died in a tragic accident, losing him placed in me a deep fear that I cannot trust others to stick around, to protect me, to provide for me — and that included God.

The more I gave in to that fear, the easier it was for me to believe the lie that I couldn't count on anyone but me. The more I believed the lie, the more deeply rooted my fear became. And I got busier — a busyness born not out of calling but out of fear of what would happen if I trusted God instead of myself.

This went for book writing too. In the spring of 2013, I was on a plane writing an outline of an article. When I stepped back to look at it, I realized it was actually the outline for a book. I tucked it away and pretended it never happened. I was scared of the challenge, scared of the unknown.

Later that year, I was in Portland, Oregon, visiting one of my best friends. She introduced me to her literary agent. After hearing my story, the agent asked me why I wasn't writing a book. I gave her a long list of the reasons why I was not interested in writing a book.

On the flight home from Portland, I asked myself the same question that the agent posed to me: Why not share my life, what I've learned and what God has done in my life? But I knew the answer. I was afraid.

Afraid of rejection. Afraid no one would publish me. Afraid that if I did get published, people would read my innermost thoughts and vulnerabilities — and laugh.

Even after I signed the contract with a publisher to write the book, I froze and didn't write a word for three months. At some point I realized I was believing the false script in my head that was telling me I wasn't good enough, smart enough, and — dare I say it — holy enough to write this book. Once I realized I was believing a lie, I could dive in and figure out the source of the fear behind the lie.

Fear is a very powerful beast, and the more we give in to the things we are afraid of, the more power our fear has in our lives. We can quote Scripture and tell ourselves all the right things about fear, but until we actually discover the source of our fear and deal with it, we will continue to give it power over us.

My fear around writing, I discovered, goes back to other thought patterns I developed as a child. I grew up with an undiagnosed learning disability that left me believing I was never as good as other students. I can still remember my teachers lecturing me and telling me that I would never get anywhere in life until I learned to focus, pay attention to details, and finish what I started. As an adult I've learned coping strategies and systems that help me overcome these difficulties, but the negative thought patterns I developed in school were much harder to break.

When you grow up hearing people tell you that you are _____ [fill in the blank], you internalize their words and, without realizing it, you begin to think those same things about yourself. Most of us have tapes playing in our heads that we have had since childhood, and at some point we began believing them. Even if they are lies.

Romans 12:2 tells us:

> Do not conform to the pattern of this world, but be trans-formed by the renewing of your mind. Then you will be able to test and approve what God's will is — his good, pleasing and perfect will.

I love this verse for two reasons. We must take control of our negative beliefs (which requires discovering their source) and transform the way we think about them. And then there is that beautiful promise: "Then you will be able to test and approve what God's will is — his good, pleasing and perfect will."

Negative thought patterns are like thought loops that we get stuck in. The weapons we fight them with are not the weapons of the world. On the contrary, our weapons have divine power to demolish strongholds. As 2 Corinthians 10:5 teaches us:

> We demolish arguments and every pretension that sets itself up against the knowledge of God, and we take captive every thought to make it obedient to Christ.

We must remember that our fears are rooted in lies from the Enemy, and that our battle is against him and not the people and circumstances in our life. Ephesians 6:12 reminds us:

For we wrestle not against flesh and blood, but against principalities, against powers, against the rulers of the darkness
of this world, against spiritual wickedness in high places.
(KJ21)

It's why the truth talk I mentioned earlier is so powerful. I
am taking the truth of God's Word and using it to destroy the
lies of the Enemy.

I'll Be Happy When . . .

During the early days of my consulting season, after I left
BlissDom, I also fell into the habit of thinking: *I'll be happy
when . . .*

In that season, my "when" was when I knew what God had
planned for me next. When he revealed his plan, I'd be happy. I
knew he wanted me to leave BlissDom, but I wanted desperately
for him to tell me what was next. And, of course, I was not going
to let myself be happy until I had answers.

As it turns out, this thought pattern is very common. Sonja
Lyubomirsky, a psychology professor from Stanford, wrote
an entire book on the myths of happiness, and she points out
that we all have the tendency to say, "I'll be happy when . . ."[13]
Sometimes we set the bar at marriage, believing we'll be happy
when we finally find our one true love. Or "I'll be happy when I
have the right job," or "I'll be happy when my health improves,"
or "I'll be happy when I have kids," and so on. I had been telling myself subconsciously that I couldn't be happy until I had
answers straight from God.

I was in a thought loop that set me up for misery. No wonder
that even when life was going great, I had my head on the table
begging God for more.

Worry about the Future

Most of us have read the Scripture about considering the lilies of the field (Matthew 6:28 KJV). How they grow beautifully but don't worry about where their next ray of sunshine is coming from. They just grow, day in, day out, sitting there being beautiful under God's watchful control and provision. And I'll be straight up with you — I want to be a lily. I want to sit right out there in that field, planted in great soil, soaking up the rays and the rain.

And I'd be a lily if it weren't for one thing. I worry about the future.

I get it. I'm not supposed to worry about the future. But I do. And I'm not alone. I have a friend who worries about just about everything in her life. She worries that her kids will get sick, so she is forever giving her kids some form of medication at the slightest hint of a sniffle. She worries her car is going to break down with her and the kids in it, so at the smallest noise or the tiniest vibration in the car, she hauls that thing off to the garage to get checked out. They don't eat out at restaurants because she's worried the kitchen isn't clean enough. Her kids all have tutors (even though they are straight-A students) because she worries they won't get into the right colleges otherwise.

Worry is different than anxiety. Anxiety is a deep sense of doom rooted in a fear that is often a lie from the Enemy. Anxiety cripples us and leaves us feeling incapable of escaping our situation. Worry, on the other hand, is our attempt to control the future. And when I say it like that, I recognize the point of the Scripture about the lilies in the field. The flowers in the field aren't sitting around worrying about their future. It's futile. Worrying about the future will not change it. The flowers are beautiful because they trust God for their provision, and he provides.

Focused on Our Flaws

I was recently at a women's event in Los Angeles where the opening speaker talked about how when she sees a beautiful woman (and the speaker herself was stunning!), she starts beating herself up mentally for eating a cookie the day before and has to force herself to stop saying horrible things to herself about her appearance.

After her talk, I noticed women in the audience were crying. I began asking the ladies at my table a question or two.

"So, that presentation was great. She's amazing. Um, sooooooo, do you think most women are that hard on themselves?"

Those LA ladies just looked at me, as if I had asked them if water was wet or if the sky was blue, as if it was the most ridiculous question anyone had ever asked in the history of the universe.

"Yes. Absolutely."

"Oh, that's nothing."

"I'm much harder on myself than she is."

"Yep. No question."

That day I learned a couple new things. I may struggle with fear, but somehow I am a woman who gives herself a lot of grace with physical appearances. I'm cool with my abundant stretch marks (I do have five kids after all!), my crazy curls that won't behave, and the laundry list of other physical imperfections.

● ● ● ● ● ●

WHEN WE FOCUS ON OUR FLAWS, WE LOSE SIGHT OF THE TRUTH THAT GOD DOES GREAT THINGS THROUGH FLAWED PEOPLE.

The habit of thinking about (and beating ourselves up over) our flaws is a deadly trap to fall into, especially for women who grow up seeing airbrushed,

Photoshopped, and surgically enhanced, idealized "role models" in magazines, on TV, and online. Whether we are focusing on our fears or focusing on our flaws (real or imagined), we are focused in the wrong place. When we stay focused on our flaws and weaknesses, we lose sight of the truth that God is the one who is great, and he does great things through flawed people.

How Negative Thoughts Make Us Busy

The more we worry, give in to fear, or think negatively about ourselves, the busier we get. We are driven to do more, be more, and prevent whatever it is we are worried about.

For me the busyness of life, the hamster wheel of trying to perform and "be good enough" (whatever that even means), kept me constantly spinning in a cycle of worry and anxiety, which in turn increased my striving, my need to do more, to accomplish more, to be more. Not only that, but my anxiety also led to a lot of fruitless frittering away of time, especially in those black holes called Pinterest and Facebook.

It wasn't until that day with my forehead on the table that I was quiet enough (or desperate enough!) to listen to God remind me who I was and who he was and why it was important for my thoughts to reflect that distinction. The difference between misery and happiness for me came not through circumstances, but through the quality of my thoughts. I needed to make a decision to walk in faith and trust God with my thoughts, not just my outward behavior.

How to Overcome Negative Thoughts

I bet you've experienced something similar with your thoughts as well. The way we think about things will determine whether we live peaceful lives, or whether we live in a busy rush to prove ourselves, please others, and strive to be and do more. So how do we break our own pattern of destructive thinking?

1. Abide in Christ

The most important way to battle negative thoughts is with the power of Christ. We do battle by using the weapons given to us all as believers: abiding (staying) in the Word of God and keeping a relationship with him through prayer and through worship.

I've learned through the years that no matter how bad I feel, no matter how negative my thoughts, if I spend time in the Word, in prayer, and in worship, I can get my thoughts right.

I may be stretching the truth, but I believe it's physically impossible to be bummed while singing "10,000 Reasons." (That's my go-to song to remember God's presence each day. Apologies to the songwriter, Matt Redman, for how I butcher it when I sing it!)

2. Stay mindful

A great way to break the impact that negative thought patterns have on you is to be aware of them. Being mindful of our own "special" thought patterns helps to remove their power in our lives.

For example, I know that I have an issue with feeling not good enough because I focus on myself too much instead of focusing on what God wants to do *to* me and *through* me. When I start focusing on my weaknesses instead of his goodness, I have to catch myself.

Think of it like this: You know those mirrors at carnivals that distort your shape and make you look crazy? They make you taller, shorter, super thin, or super heavy? We could look in those mirrors and feel depressed or confused by what we see in them (especially the ones that make us heavier!). But as adults, we realize that what we see in those mirrors is just an illusion. Our reflection has no power over us because it's not the truth. In the same way, when we stay mindfully aware of our own illusions (fears, anxieties, shame, and worries), they lose their power over us.

3. Surround yourself with positive friends

The term *emotional contagion* means that our emotions are so contagious that emotions between people can actually converge. Scientists recently proved that even the emotions of our social media friends can affect us.[14] If emotional contagion happens via social media, just imagine how powerful it is in real life!

The negative emotions, thoughts, and words from others are like secondhand smoke. You may not be the one smoking (or doing the negative thinking), but you suffer from the toxic effects all the same.

Toxic people breathe toxic results into your life. Positive people breathe positive results. Of course in real life you will find yourself with people who can be difficult to get along with. You may have coworkers and family members who tend to be negative. Obviously you can't just write those people out of your life. But you can be wise with relationships and the people you give your time and emotional energy to.

4. Focus on the discipline of gratitude

A discipline is a focused practice that brings about a positive behavioral change. (Yes, I know that was geeky and scientific, but hang in there with me.) Therefore, the discipline of gratitude is the focused practice of being grateful in order to change our behavior for the better.

My friend Jeff Goins wrote:

One of the curses of living in such a fast-paced society is that we tend to take things for granted. We overlook everyday blessings, oblivious to the fact that life itself is a gift. And if we're not careful, we can find ourselves rushing through each day, less and less grateful, which is no way to live.[15]

He goes on to compare this curse as the sickness of ingratitude, which eventually "takes root in our hearts, where it can be hard to shake."[16]

Training ourselves to be grateful is a discipline. Make no mistake about that. It takes time and loads of practice to develop gratitude. I have my time in the evenings with the boys to think of things I'm grateful for, but during the day I also take time to think of three people I can show gratitude or love for. I will then text or write a short email (just two to four sentences) to say how much I appreciate them, or I'll have a short conversation with them expressing thanks. The whole process takes less than fifteen minutes, but it is one of the happiest things (for me and everyone else!) that I do all day.

What if you regularly told people how grateful you are for them or something they have done? My guess is it would transform your life. It did mine!

Practicing gratitude can be a battle (much like any other discipline). The Bible is very clear that this war is not fought on a physical plane, but is a spiritual battle. Ephesians 6:12 says:

For we wrestle not against flesh and blood, but against principalities, against powers, against the rulers of the darkness of this world, against spiritual wickedness in high places. (KJ21)

Learning to take our thoughts captive and focus them on the One who has control of our lives is a discipline worth developing.

Grace and Gratitude Are Our Good Soil

Once I woke up to the reality that I could trust God and his promises for me, I began to love my work as a consultant and business coach. The same days I used to dread became joy filled even though nothing changed except my mindset. Through the renewing of my mind, the old fears and negativity gave way to gratitude and happiness.

In order for any plant to grow and produce fruit, it must be deeply rooted in good soil. For us, as believers, grace and gratitude are our good soil. We break busy and find our peace in a world of worry when we live our lives in the knowledge that God loves us and is in control of our lives. By recognizing and releasing our fears to God, by letting go of our white-knuckled hold on the details of our lives, and by walking in the belief that he loves us and will provide for us, we find peace and comfort.

Action Steps

1. Identify a destructive thought pattern that plagues you. Write it down.

2. Find a Scripture that counteracts your destructive thoughts, replacing them with God's truth. Memorize it.

3. Ask yourself if you have ever thought, "I'll be happy when …" Do you believe the lie that you can't *really* be happy and have peace in your life until some benchmark is reached?

4. Every day think of three things and people you are grateful for. Write them down and, if possible, tell those people you are grateful for them.

SIX

TRADITIONS

*Finding Your Groove in a
World of Expectations*

I love the Christmas season. Not just the day itself, but the whole entire Christmas season. As soon as I can get away with it, my car is filled with Christmas music, the smell of peppermint mochas, and piles of random hats and gloves. But it was not so long ago that I did not love the Christmas season. Oh, I still loved Christmas music, peppermint mochas, and decorating our trees. I just didn't love everything else that came with the season: the shopping, the parties, the baking, the cards, the concerts, the obligations that seemed endless. "'Tis the season to be jolly," my foot!

One particularly notable December a few years back, after making my Christmas to-do list filled with class parties and cookie swaps and party-dress shopping and family photos and Christmas cards, I snapped. I couldn't take one more second of the rat race Christmas had become. I couldn't bring myself to tell the people in my life that I wasn't playing the game of Christmas Crazy anymore, so instead, I told the masses, via the Internet. I wrote an article called "Why I Won't Be Getting You a Christmas Present" for my online column for Disney.

In my article, I wrote about growing up in a family and community where the women often worked hard to be all things to all people, especially during the holidays. From baking to gift wrapping to perfect hair to coordinated outfits ... no detail was too small to ignore and hardly a moment went by when these women weren't working trying to make sure everything was perfect for everyone. As an adult I understand what a massive task that was. And while I will always appreciate their effort, I am most definitely not following in their footsteps. I learned that when you try to be all things to all people, what you really end up doing is cheating yourself out of happiness and peace. I wanted to give myself and every other mother on the planet permission to take a different approach to the holidays if they so desired.

I wrote:

> To start, I've got five kids. Right there that's no less than 25 teachers, a dozen coaches, countless parties, Sunday school instructors, etc. If I added up all of the people affiliated with my kids that I'm "supposed" to bake cookies for or give gifts to, I'd never have time to breathe, let alone enjoy myself.
>
> Even if I didn't have any children, this season is full of obligations ... parties, gift and cookie exchanges, Secret Santa this or that, party invitations around every corner, etc. It's all too much.

I went on to say exactly how we had simplified our holidays into a time of year that was truly meaningful to our family and a time we truly enjoyed.

So the next time you sigh with exasperation and stress because you haven't even ordered your holiday cards yet let alone sent them ... remember this. *You don't have to be all things to all people.* Just be the best you to the people who matter the most.[17]

When the article was published, I sheepishly shared it on Facebook and Twitter, secretly worried that my friends who have the hospitality gene would think I was being harsh, or worse, making fun of them (which I wasn't!). A few friends and followers thought just that and wrote,

"But I love baking, and sewing gifts and doing Elf on the Shelf."

Or

"Throwing Christmas parties and giving gifts is my love language."

To those friends, I said, "God bless you. You make up for people like me, and please invite me to your party ... I'll bring some store-bought cookies and pie."

Kathie Lee and Hoda Interview Scrooge

But two days after my article posted, I received a note at midnight from a friend at the *Today Show.* We had met years ago when she spoke at BlissDom. She had seen my article on Facebook and said she wanted to discuss how moms feel overwhelmed during the holidays. I needed to fly up to New York City *the next day* and be on the show the following morning.

My first thought was, *I was nervous about an article on the Internet. Now I am going on live television to tell five million people that I'm Scrooge!*

My second thought was, *What the heck! Yes!* That night, my biggest concern was, "How do I share my message in a way that will help women be gentle to themselves and stop the madness around the holidays?"

Who am I kidding? I wish I could say that was my biggest concern, but it wasn't. I was primarily worried about my roots — the ones growing on top of my head! I was overdue to get them done and, of course, I wouldn't have time before leaving for New York.

I Googled, "How to cover your roots," and discovered there were several products available so I could do the job at home. I stopped by my local beauty store on the way to the airport the next morning and said, "I need some stuff to cover my roots. A makeup stick or spray or something … I read about it on the Internet."

"Yes, honey. Over here," the nice sales lady said as she guided me to the correct aisle.

I found three different products. One looked just like a foundation stick, one like a mascara, and one was a spray. I asked her which would be best.

"Well, honey, why are you in such a hurry?" she asked without the least bit of judgment in her voice.

"Um, I'm going to be on a video," I said, then realized I sounded crazy. But the damage was already done.

"A video?" she said in an overly loud voice. "A video? Honey, what kind of video you gonna be on?"

I wish I could accurately portray with words just how deeply Southern this woman was, and I'm from the South, so that's saying something. She was a picture straight out of *Steel Magnolias*, big hair and charm all rolled up in a sweet Southern drawl that made every statement seem so much more interesting than it really was.

"Well, not really a video," I said. "I'm going to be on the *Today Show* in the morning and I'm worried about my roots. I'm on the way to the airport. I need help."

That sweet lady looked at me as if I had lost my mind.

I expected her to say in her loud Southern voice, "The *Today Show*? The *Todayyyyyy Show*?" But she didn't utter a word. We just stood there in awkward silence as she stared at me, her mouth slightly open, her hands on her hips and a look of genuine concern on her face. I wasn't sure if she was concerned that I was a lunatic or if my root problems were too big for such a quick-fix treatment.

Finally, she said, "Well, honey, I gotta tell you. If you haven't ever used any of these, I don't want you to now. Your roots ain't too bad, but you may end up looking way worse if you try to cover it yourself. Just get yourself on that plane and stop worrying about your roots. You're gonna be just fine, sugar."

So that's what I did.

Nashville to New York. Airport to hotel. Boom. I was ready.

Have you ever worried when you were falling asleep that you would sleep late and miss something important in the morning? (As we have already determined, I'm not good with early mornings.)

I had two wake-up calls, my phone programmed, and I had even paid my oldest son $3 to call me at 5 a.m. I had received a call from the show the night before telling me to bring my wardrobe options with me, and they'd help me choose which to wear. Um, yeah, that would have been great information to have *before* I left Tennessee. Simple dresser that I am, I wore all black from head to toe. I brought only one outfit with me. Gulp.

So, with all the confidence I could muster, I put on my dress, did my hair, applied my makeup, and headed off for Rockefeller Center and my debut on the *Today Show*. Apparently, most guests walk over to the studio and get their hair and makeup done there. But I decided to apply my own and then let the makeup artist show me what I needed to change. (How else would I know what I was doing wrong if I didn't show her, right?)

In the makeup chair, I learned that my eyebrows needed pencil (who knew?) and that my makeup needed contouring (how did I make it thirty-seven years without contouring skills?). The hairdresser offered to straighten my hair. I politely declined, but I did ask her if my roots were okay. She chuckled and said she didn't notice them.

Isn't it funny how much time we waste focused on a perceived weakness or flaw in ourselves that no one else even notices?

Behind the scenes, Kathie Lee and Hoda are the nicest, funniest ladies ever, and the *Today Show* team is professional and lovely. I did my best to act like I knew what I was doing and that I was on TV all the time. I pretended to be unimpressed in the green room with the celebrities all around me. This was just normal life.

"Don't faint, snort-laugh, throw up, or freeze," I told myself. "And no wide-eyed thing."

You think I'm joking, but in my early days of being interviewed on local TV morning shows, I apparently made this wild wide-eyed look whenever I was nervous. I made it often enough that when I called a friend who is in the business, her one coaching tip was, "Don't do the wide-eyed thing."

Once I was on the show with Kathie Lee and Hoda, I chatted about how I grew up watching the women in my family laboriously produce giant holiday celebrations and never actually enjoy themselves. I didn't want to continue that legacy. I shared that I want holidays I can enjoy and discussed how our family developed new traditions that fit us in this season of life.

The whole segment was just a few minutes, and when it was over, you've never seen a happier girl. But I began to worry about what would happen when NBC posted the video. I'd probably be raked over the coals in the comment section.

Instead, when I was safely home in Nashville, I started

receiving emails, notes, and messages saying how much people enjoyed hearing me say, "You don't have to be all things to all people." It's as if we all need someone to say that out loud.

Sometimes our lives are full of busyness because traditions make us believe that is how it *has* to be done. You know, when you've *always* done something a certain way, it's hard to break free from that — at least without feeling guilty that you aren't doing it anymore. But just because we live in a world of seemingly endless expectations doesn't mean we have to live up to them.

> • • • • • •
> **JUST BECAUSE WE LIVE IN A WORLD OF SEEMINGLY ENDLESS EXPECTATIONS DOESN'T MEAN WE HAVE TO LIVE UP TO THEM.**

The Importance of Traditions

Now, I'm not bashing all traditions. I'm just saying not all traditions are healthy for everyone. Family traditions, when done well, for example, give families a greater sense of security and make everyone happier.

Traditions of our faith are also vitally important. Long before the written Word of God was given to man, the children of God passed down events of biblical history and tenets of their faith by celebrating those events in the same manner year after year. They passed on those traditions to their children and their grandchildren and their great-grandchildren. And we do the same thing today. Some of our traditions are based on Scripture and are vital to our lives as Christians: meeting together regularly (Hebrews 10:25), celebrating the Lord's Supper (1 Corinthians 11:17–34), and praying and reading the Bible (Deuteronomy 6:4–8), for example.

But there are many traditions and activities of the faith that are both cultural and optional. Depending on your church culture and interests, you may attend potlucks and teach Sunday school, or you may work in a food pantry or take part in a local prison ministry. Every church has its own traditions and ministries. The trouble comes when you think you need to do it all (or do a certain thing everyone else does) just to prove your commitment to Christ, when Jesus himself isn't calling you to do that thing "everyone else does."

If anyone knew about the burden of tradition, it was Jesus. He knew all about the religious burdens the Pharisees had placed on the people, and he publicly rebuked the Pharisees for doing so. In Matthew 15:1–20, Jesus pretty much puts the smackdown on the religious rulers for being more concerned about tradition than they were about worshiping God and having a relationship with him.

• • • • • •

TRADITIONS DONE FOR THE WRONG REASONS SHACKLE US TO UNREALISTIC EXPECTATIONS AND A WHOLE LOT OF UNNECESSARY BUSYWORK.

Hear me say this: Tradition is not a bad thing. But like any good thing, done with the wrong motivation (namely guilt and the pride of keeping up with the Joneses), traditions can shackle us to unrealistic expectations and a whole lot of unnecessary busywork. If we think we have to do everything and be all things to all people, before we know it, we will be stuck on a hamster wheel, going nowhere fast.

I Blame Pinterest

Traditions and rituals (and I'm not just talking about Christmas ones) are best when they add to our lives, not become a source of extra work, busyness, and headaches.

After many missteps and mistakes in finding my groove in a

world of expectations, I have learned to chill out about things. I have kids in all ages and stages of preadult lives, so when it comes to raising children, I've learned to take life at the pace it comes.

In other words, I'm chill.

That is ...

Until ...

I get on Pinterest.

And then I am overcome with the need to create, recycle, upcycle, do, glue, paint, design, decorate, make and bake, all for the sake of "making memories" with my children. And when I'm done with all of that, I'm supposed to dream, surprise, inspire, delight, protect, teach, nurture, discipline, and feed them!

I tell you, I thought I had it all together until I got on Pinterest. As it turns out, I am a slug for a mom. I don't know how to cook organic food from scratch. I'll never have buns or abs of steel. I can't braid my hair in a fishtail-bun-upswept-messy-updo. Can't paint the map from *The Hobbit* on my fingernails. Will never decorate with mason jars. And I don't know how to make a single thing from an old wooden pallet.

Is it too crazy to announce that Pinterest has ruined birthday parties forever and ever? It has. Before Pinterest, you could have a flat birthday cake with candles and maybe even some characters on top. Now birthday cakes have to be tiered with lava flowing from them or Elsa and Anna shooting icicles or they won't be Instagrammable. Yeah, I said it. (But, for the record, I do Instagram our sheet cakes. Fight the power, ladies.)

In fact, have you noticed how the whole birthday party game has been upped in the last few years? We used to invite kids over and go to a fast-food play land or meet at a park to celebrate a kid's birthday. Not anymore. Now we have ponies, themed occasions, and Cirque de Soleil. Okay, maybe not Cirque, yet. But you know it's coming!

Don't get me wrong. I'm not saying big elaborate parties are a bad thing, if that is what you love to do. I enjoy going to parties where they've rented a petting zoo, made the Roman Colosseum out of marshmallows, and have massive goodie bags with toys and candy. I support anyone who wants to throw an epic party. What keeps me from finding my own groove is when I start believing that I also need to throw an epic party or I won't measure up.

Birthday parties in our family are low-key. I explain to the kids that we have a birthday budget and that budget can be spent on a party or gifts. So far we have one boy out of five who some years wants a party instead of gifts. I know, I know, I've been lucky. And if a party had to happen at our house, you better believe there's no Cirque budget, and any expectation or hopes of big goodie bags will be dashed quickly.

Wouldn't it be great if we could say freely, "You do your thing. Make that life-sized Olaf out of marshmallows and hire princesses to come over. That's awesome. But I'm cool not to do those things."

After my visit to the *Today Show* and the conversations I've had with hundreds of women since, I think we really *are* cool with not doing those things. Meaning, we are okay not to live out and continue (or pick up) traditions that don't mean anything to us. But we are still afraid to find our own groove and live in it because we are worried someone might judge us and find us lacking.

● ● ● ● ● ●

I SAY, "BAKE YOUR CAKE, BUY YOUR CAKE, DON'T HAVE A CAKE AT ALL!"

I say, "Bake your cake, buy your cake, don't have a cake at all!" We are all adults and none of us have the time to care or judge how anyone else is doing it. That's the world I want to live in. (But if you do have cake, please invite me over. I love cake.)

Great Expectations

When I asked my friends what expectations they felt they had to live up to, the answers were both telling and hilarious:

- "I must plan awesome family vacations that we will talk about for generations to come."
- "I have to have lovely, professional family photos taken every year."
- "I can only feed my baby organic, locally sourced food or I'm not being a good mother."
- "Even though I have a family of three, I have to drive a car that seats at least seven people just in case I need to haul a sports team somewhere or drive for a school or church trip."
- "I must dress like a model every day. Those 'outfit of the day' #OOTD photos all over Pinterest and Instagram are crazy. Who can keep up?"

I get exhausted just looking at the list. The thing about any of these "must-do's" is they are all fine things if you're doing them because you love them and are called to do them. But if not, you're in danger of living someone else's life, instead of experiencing the uniquely wonderful, beautifully crafted life Jesus planned for *you*.

Why Traditions Need to Be Flexible

Depending on our stage of life, the traditions we continue, start, change, or stop will vary. I have a friend whose mother-in-law decorates every single room of her house for Christmas. Literally every single room in the house. But her mother-in-law is retired, has no children living at home, loves decorating, and loves having people over for the holidays. Not only that, her husband's family has family Christmas traditions that include four different "must-do" events each year, a certain way they wrap their gifts, and even specific foods they have on Christmas Eve.

My friend, on the other hand, has four small children, a full-time job, and almost no time to herself, much less time to carry on all of the traditions of her husband's family. Overwhelmed with the guilt of not being able to manage it all, she talked with her mother-in-law. Much to her surprise, her mother-in-law said, "When I was your age with my four small children and a full-time job, do you think I did all these things? No way. I did well to buy presents, get them wrapped, and even *have* a tree, much less decorate my whole house. But I have time now, so I do the things I enjoy."

● ● ● ● ● ●

TRADITIONS DON'T HAVE TO BE EXPECTATIONS.

You have to allow yourself to do the things you enjoy, to carry on the traditions that are meaningful to you, and be okay to know that your children, family, and friends might not carry on all of the traditions that are meaningful to you.

Sisters from Two Thousand Years Ago

When I think of living according to expectations and tradition, I cannot help but think about Jesus' friends Mary and Martha. When I think of Mary and Martha, for some reason I think of Jan and Marcia Brady from the classic TV show *The Brady Bunch*.

Marcia was the bubbly Brady, the popular one. She was everyone's friend, kind, generous in every way. Then there was Jan. Jan was a great girl. Helpful, always concerned about pleasing those around her. Always making sure everyone was okay. Always doing what was expected of her. But man, was she tired of living in Marcia's shadow. It was always all about Marcia. Marcia, Marcia, Marcia.

In my mind, here's how the story of the biblical sisters unfolded. Jesus and his disciples came into town. Mary, the bubbly sister, everyone's friend, the relationship builder, wanted nothing more than to hang out with Jesus. She wanted to spend time with him, hear about his travels, listen to his teaching. Oh, she could have listened to him teach forever.

And Martha? Martha had her to-do list made before Jesus ever got there. Between the time that word had reached them of his impending arrival and the time he arrived, Martha had planned an incredible banquet for Jesus and his disciples. She Instagrammed the table, pinned the best recipes, and even Snapchatted a few of her closest friends about all the hard work she was putting into the dinner for Jesus. And you know she hashtagged it all with #Blessed #DinnerWithJesus.

Once Jesus arrived, Martha was in the kitchen — all pleased with herself and how well things were going — when she heard Mary's laughter wafting from the living room. What in the world was Mary doing out there with the men? Didn't she know there was work to be done? That chicken wasn't going to fry itself! So Martha walked out into the room where Jesus was teaching, and when she saw Mary sitting at his feet, she blew up!

According to Luke 10:40–42, she said, "Lord, don't you care that my sister has left me to do the work by myself? Tell her to help me!"

And the Lord answered, "Martha, Martha, Martha [*sorry, couldn't resist*], you are worried and upset about many things, but few things are needed — or indeed only one. Mary has chosen what is better, and it will not be taken away from her."

Martha behaved out of expectations and tradition instead of

spending that precious time in the company of those she loved. I daresay she might even have allowed a little bit of pride to enter into her efforts. She wasn't just making a meal for a guest. She was cooking for *Jesus*, and it was going to be the best dinner anyone had ever cooked for him — ever.

When we become overwhelmed with all the things we think we have to do, and when we allow our pride to enter into the mix, it's easy to feel frazzled and even resentful, just like Martha did that day. That's why Jesus told her that Mary had chosen the only needed thing. Mary had chosen peace and time with those she loved.

Tweaking Traditions

Like Martha, you may find yourself caught in the trap of expectations and traditions, and you may need some help to escape the shackles. So here are a few pointers to tweak those traditions so they fit you, your family, your current stage of life — and your faith in Jesus.

1. Follow Jesus first

There's probably no greater "tradition" to buck than that of social norms. Challenging those norms can exact a heavy toll as we work to please God before culture.

The past three years I have worked from my home office while Mark has worked inside the home, being full-time dad (and a million other roles) to our sons. This is a decision we made together, based on the season of our life and the direction we heard from God. But it was not an easy decision. It goes against old-fashioned social norms and requires us to explain our choices often to family, friends, business colleagues, and even strangers. It's exhausting.

It has a financial cost too. Mark could easily make a great income that would give us the ability to have more conveniences and luxuries. But he is doing what God called him to do. No amount of money is worth more than our obedience to God.

We don't have a road map or a guidebook for this. It's confusing. Some days we both think it would be way easier for me to work part time at home with the kids and give up my speaking and travel schedule and Mark to work full time outside the home. Those roles are more familiar to us. But since our roles have reversed, I've had to learn to hand over the reins of running the household and to let go of the mommy guilt I sometimes feel. And who knows (only God knows) what our future holds? Down the road, the Lord might call us to reverse our roles again.

Every tradition that we keep or discard, whether related to Christmas, birthdays, weddings, or even those related to social norms, needs to start with Jesus first. What is he calling us to do? How can we show our love for him first? Then we ask ourselves, "How can I best show my love to others (including myself)?" (Remember, the two greatest commandments recorded in Matthew 22:36–40, tell us to love God above all, and love your neighbor as yourself.) In our case, following Jesus and loving our boys and ourselves led to a nontraditional answer, one we live out in faith every single day.

2. Drop (or don't pick up) the traditions you don't enjoy

When my oldest was a toddler and I was pregnant with our second son, Jack, we moved to Memphis. It was the first move away from all my friends and family, and I was focused on finding new friends.

After finding a new church and joining a Bible study, I noticed the ladies also met together each week and took a sewing class. They made smocked rompers for their kids to wear. My toddler wore regular boy clothes, but I quickly planned on joining the class, learning to sew, and making that boy some rompers. This was the tradition in the suburbs of Memphis. Here's the kicker, though: I hate sewing. I can barely sew on a button. If something needs hemming, I might as well throw it away. I have actually stapled the hem in a pair of pants. But I was ready to take that class just to fit in.

The Sunday after I signed up for the sewing class was Easter. On the drive home from the Easter egg hunt, my husband said, "Babe, please don't put Justin in those one-piece outfits with embroidered baby ducks."

Mark is from Pittsburgh and not used to the traditions of the South — still, after living here for almost twenty years. I started laughing and admitted I was planning on taking a sewing class to start making those exact rompers.

Mark said, "But, babe, you hate sewing. Why would you do that?"

"To make friends," I admitted sheepishly.

"But you are friends with them already. You are in Bible study together. Why do you have to start sewing girly outfits to stay friends with them?"

This was my wake-up call. I had put the expectation on myself that to be accepted and keep my new set of friends, I needed to change who I was.

Taking a class to learn to do something I detested was not beneficial to anyone. So I left that tradition to my new friends, and no sewing machines, baby-duck-embroidered rompers, or feelings were hurt in the making of this story.

3. Find an easier way to keep the tradition

My friend Meredith is genius when it comes to customizing traditions. When I asked about how other people manage expectations and traditions, she said, "We totally skip Christmas cards and opt for New Year's cards instead. Somehow, not dealing with them during the holiday season makes them more fun and relaxed for us."

She still does her annual card, she just found a way to make the process easier. I love this! By customizing traditions we love, we can take them from being a chore to something we cherish.

4. Look for a win-win solution

Most things that require give-and-take end up best when we look for the win-win solution. My friend Lisa found the win-win solution to managing the expectations of her relatives and in-laws, and it kept everyone happy!

"We don't spend Christmas Day or Eve with both sides of the family anymore. My family and my in-laws live equal distances away from my house, one side of the family north of us and one side south of us. Our first Christmas together, my husband and I tried to spend Christmas with both sides of the family, and we spent more time in the car driving than we did visiting! After that, we told our families that one side gets us for Thanksgiving and the other side gets us for Christmas. It flip-flops every year."

It's easy to get stuck in the trap of thinking, "This is how we have to do it." When we change our thinking to look for the win-win, it helps us figure out how to change (or stop!) traditions that keep us too busy.

5. Give yourself permission to disappoint

When all else fails, give yourself permission to disappoint someone (including yourself). Pray about it, then let it go.

A friend of mine was planning her wedding and, in the midst of the chaos of planning, she almost had a nervous breakdown. Between all the "must-do's" on her mom's list and the "must-do's" on her mother-in-law's list, there was not much room left for what she and her fiancé wanted. In the end, she and her husband-to-be had to sit down with their families and gently let them know that while they wanted to honor each of their families' traditions, it was their wedding, their special day, and they were going to plan it. The conversation and days that followed weren't without some tears (it's never fun to disappoint those we love), but the wedding was beautiful, and all the truly meaningful components were there.

Expectations — sometimes put on us by others, and sometimes ones we put on ourselves — have to be managed well to break the cycle of busy in our lives. Finding our groove in a world of expectations means not only asking ourselves tough questions but also turning to Jesus to ask him, "What's truly important here? What do you want me to do right now?" When we purposefully follow Jesus instead of blindly following tradition or succumbing to our own or someone else's expectations, we will find peace and purpose even in the midst of a world of crazy.

● ● ● ● ● ●

WHEN WE PURPOSEFULLY FOLLOW JESUS INSTEAD OF BLINDLY FOLLOWING TRADITION OR SUCCUMBING TO EXPECTATIONS, WE WILL FIND PEACE.

Action Steps

1. What tradition do you keep that you secretly wish you could change or drop?

2. Evaluate your faith traditions. Are there activities you are doing purely out of "tradition" rather than out of a genuine calling to do those things? Pray and ask Jesus what he would have you do for him.

3. Look at an upcoming traditional event (birthday, holiday, wedding, small group meeting, dinner party, etc.) and look for some way to tweak it to better reflect your available time and energy.

SEVEN

TIME

Finding Your Rhythm in a World of Overwhelm

Don't you love the start of a new year? Next to Christmas, New Year's Day has always been one of my favorite times of the year. I think I love it so much because it feels so rife with possibility. It feels so, well ... new.

For years, I was like most of the millions of people in the world. I spent the last month of the year overeating, overcommitting, and overspending, all the while making resolutions for how I would change my life in the upcoming year. And let me assure you, I can make a resolution like nobody's business. I have most likely set some world records with my resolutions, records like "Fastest Broken Resolution" or "Most Likely to Break a Leg While Breaking a Resolution." My resolutions normally last a few hours, a day, or even a few days if I'm feeling really inspired.

It's true. I have a long list of messed-up New Year's resolutions on my resolution résumé. One year I decided to give up gluten because it was the cool thing to do. Everyone, it seemed, was gluten-free, so even though I'm not allergic to gluten, I gave it up, thinking it would help me lay off the carbs a bit. It worked, and I actually made it seven months before returning to my love of all things bread-based. As far as resolutions go, it was one of my more successful (or at the very least, longest lasting).

Then there was the year I decided to start running. I ran on January 1 and immediately twisted my ankle. Then, while hopping around on my husband's old crutches, I pinched a nerve in my neck. I ended up with a neck brace for three weeks. Seriously, I wish I was kidding!

Lesson learned: I am not to be trusted with crutches.

Another time, I decided that I was going to get more rest because, well, *that* is surely something a mother of five sons is bound to need. You can just guess how long that resolution lasted. (But in my defense, this one was kind of out of my control from the get-go.)

After a decade of false starts at New Year's, I decided to find a resolution I could actually keep. One that would actually change my life.

Are you ready to hear what it was?

I decided to figure out how I spent my time. That was my whole resolution. I wrote it down. **Figure out how I am spending my time.** Followed by, **Make a time diary.**

Wait. Don't close the book.

Keep reading and let me tell you what happened. I promise it was life changing for me and will be life changing for you.

Life by the Calendar

Most of us want to manage our time well. We want to go to bed at night feeling we accomplished something that day, kept our priorities straight, and still have freedom and flexibility to have fun. It sounds so easy, doesn't it? Yet managing our time is one of those things that we all wish we could do better.

For years I tried to manage my time better by buying a new

planner or new productivity app and meticulously planning my day. Unfortunately, "life by the calendar" always left me feeling a little tense and mildly guilty when I didn't keep up with my intensely planned life. The real world had a way of derailing my calendar. New calls popped up during the day, kids got sick, workloads varied. I never seemed to be able to get in a good rhythm, and I always ended up frustrated and overwhelmed. In short, my well-planned but incredibly rigid schedule just didn't work.

I was running my one-woman consulting company and was working like a crazy woman to get it all done every day. I was actively shopping for productivity systems and accessories (stress shopping anyone?) and decided that instead of buying new gadgets, I would do something much smarter — I'd figure out how I actually spent my time. I knew I couldn't fix my time-management issues until I knew what got me into the mess in the first place. No productivity system or pretty planner was going to help me until I knew what in the world I was spending my time on.

WHEN WE LIVE IN A WORLD OF CRAZY BUSY, IT IS SOMETIMES OF OUR OWN MAKING.

I did some research to discover if there was "an app for that." As luck would have it, there was. And after three months of using an app on my computer to automatically chart how I spent my time online, I was shocked at how much time I wasted with little things that weren't really important.[18] In addition to the app I used to chart my time online, I also used my planner (yes, I still used one, but just in a different way) to record how I spent my time offline. I discovered that I lived in a world of crazy busy, and much to my dismay, it was of my own making! I was wasting half of my day on little time wasters (hello, five-minute video on baby sloths on YouTube!) and lots of seemingly urgent tasks.

What was most surprising to me was that those seemingly urgent tasks weren't as important as I'd made them out to be.

The Tyranny of the Urgent

Once I started my work life in the online world, both as a blogger and as the cofounder of BlissDom Events and cofounder and CCO (Chief Creative Officer) of Blissful Media Group, I became accustomed to always being online and "always working." Thanks to the ease of accessibility through my phone, even my "off hours" were spent working. There were conference calls from football sidelines, work-related email catch-up from the car on the way home from church, and constant connection via social media. Even when I stopped BlissDom, my habits continued. My time diary showed me I had become a slave to work, and my health, happiness, and family suffered for it.

I was a slave to the tyranny of the urgent, and urgency was a ruthless taskmaster.

If you are unfamiliar with the phrase "tyranny of the urgent,"[19] it describes a life of constant tension between the urgent (constantly putting out little fires and checking off the to-do lists) and the truly important (our relationship with God and the bigger priorities of life). The problem is that many important tasks (such as getting adequate sleep, spending quiet time with God every day, and working toward our big goals in life) don't seem urgent enough to demand our immediate attention, while urgent tasks (like stopping the kids from bickering over who gets the toy first or answering that text) aren't always important.

But urgency is not patient.

Urgency has no boundaries.

Urgency is demanding and controlling.

Urgency is a terrible tyrant. She demands that you give her 100 percent of your attention 100 percent of the time.

Maybe you have felt the demanding taunts of urgency in your everyday life. You want to finish your Bible study, but those piles of laundry must get done. You want to sit down at the end of a long day at work and read a book to your little ones, but you can't take your mind off the emails you know you didn't answer.

My time diary showed me that a lot of urgent things were taking my time, but they weren't all that important. I had to make some changes. With my new career focus on consulting and coaching clients, I had to drop the bad habits I had carried over from the events company, habits that had me online 24/7. I couldn't help other people find success until I found my own rhythm and stopped living life overwhelmed by what felt urgent.

My first few months as a business coach revealed to me a mindset that permeates the business world. People think success in business (and in life) is all about adding in some cool tricks, taking out a few things that don't work, following a strategic recipe, and BOOM! Success follows.

The truth is that whether you are the manager of a home, CEO of a company, or a busy entrepreneur, your ability to be successful is equal to your physical and mental health and your ability to manage your time and energy.

Around the time I started tracking my own time, I started giving my coaching clients an exercise that proved to be as eye opening as it was frustrating. The exercise was simple: pay attention to how you spend an average day and write down how you spend your time. Do this for one week and look for the patterns. From numerous clients, two main themes came forth:

"Wow, I don't have any spare time. This is crazy."

Or ...

"I watch more TV [or spend more time on Facebook or

Pinterest] than I thought I did. Whoa. Thirty hours a week on TV, really?"

I knew if my clients didn't discover how they really spent their time, they would not begin to see real progress in their work. My clients who were overscheduled and overcommitted would continue to feel overwhelmed, and the ones who watched thirty hours of TV every week would continue to tell themselves that they didn't have extra time for *anything*.

Time seems like a small thing to steward well, yet it is something we often squander without even realizing it. When we are able to steward what is in our hands on a small scale, we'll be prepared to steward greater success and responsibilities in our lives.

Setting Goals and Priorities

You and I were made for more than the habits we sometimes settle for, such as watching hours of reality TV, browsing Facebook, and playing Candy Crush on our iPhones. Instead we should be doing more life-giving activities that make us happy and help us grow into who we are meant to be. But we will never get to those activities if we don't first set our goals and our priorities.

Think of your last vacation. What helped you arrive at your destination? First, you chose a place, say, Florida. Then you chose a time: spring break. Then you picked out a place to stay and things to do: Disney! Then you packed ... and so on. The simple goal of "vacation" initiated a whole succession of choices and activities that allowed you to reach your destination.

In the same way, we will never get to the most important destinations in life without first envisioning them, then prioritizing and scheduling the activities that get us there.

Want close family relationships? Perhaps you will prioritize the family dinner, which will mean planning, shopping, and cooking meals.

Want a successful career? Perhaps you will prioritize a full-time job and hire someone to clean the house or cook the meals.

Want to finish that project? Perhaps you will get up early, turn off the phone, eat at your desk, and avoid people for the day!

When you know what your goals and priorities are

WE HAVE TO MAKE SURE WE SPEND TIME DOING THINGS THAT ACTUALLY GET US CLOSER TO OUR GOALS.

(in both the short and long run), you can decide if a certain activity will get you closer or farther away from that goal. Make sure you spend time doing things that get you closer to your goals.

Living life by the tyranny of the urgent is often just a case of jumbled priorities. My favorite saying used to be, "I just need a few more hours in each day!" But what I learned was that I didn't need more time. I needed to focus on my goals and what I needed to do to reach them.

I sometimes think we must be amusing to God, running around trying to do so much, constantly trying to find our rhythm in a world of being overwhelmed, when the reality is, if we'd slow down, do fewer "urgent" things, and ask him about what is important (what our goals in life should be), we might be surprised by what he could accomplish through us. After all, Ephesians 3:20 tells us he "is able to do immeasurably more than all we ask or imagine, according to his power that is at work within us."

Immeasurably more than all we ask or imagine according to his power that is at work within us. As Christians, we are not limited by what we think we can do. No, God has great plans and a destiny for us all, and his power is already at work within us. When we steward our day-to-day lives well, we can live the life he has planned for us.

Jeremiah 29:11 is a verse many of us recite as casually as we would order a glass of sweet tea in a restaurant in the South. " 'For I know the plans I have for you,' declares the LORD, 'plans to prosper you and not to harm you, plans to give you hope and a future.' " When we let this verse sink into our hearts, when we focus on the good work God has planned in us, it's easier to stop doing the things that aren't beneficial for us.

Think of stewarding your time well as a spiritual discipline. If we stay in a cycle of busyness because we can't manage our time well, can't say no because the discomfort in the moment hurts, or believe (falsely) that we are "good" Christians only when we say yes to everything, we will forever be overwhelmed, never having the time or energy to live out our God-given destiny. But if we ask God's help in setting our goals and priorities, he will show us where to spend our time — and help us to prune the distracting activities that get in the way.

Setting Boundaries on Your Time

Although my New Year's resolution that year was simply to "figure out how I was spending my time," I had to do something with my findings if my resolution was going to have any meaning. I started by setting boundaries on my time, cutting out and saying no to nonessential activities. Here's how:

1. Make a stop-doing list

Our lives have gotten so cluttered up with things we think we "should" do, we can't figure out what we were *meant* to do.

Read that last sentence again. Slowly. It's important. (I'm not kidding. Read it again. Slowly.)

Let your life be about what you are meant to do, not full of what you think you should do. This starts with your daily decisions about how you spend your time.

The best way to identify what you want/need to stop doing is by asking yourself these questions:

1. What is sucking the life right out of me?
2. Does this activity get me closer to reaching my goals in life?

For me, when I identified what I needed to stop doing, I found two areas that were sucking the life out of me and keeping me from reaching my goals: phone calls and meetings.

I decided to stop answering my phone when I didn't know the number. This was huge for me. Sometimes it was someone who was very sweet, who had gotten my number from a mutual friend and wanted some counseling or coaching. Calls like this would come in once a week, and instead of doing what I needed to do, I would spend thirty to sixty minutes on a call.

> **LET YOUR LIFE BE ABOUT WHAT YOU ARE MEANT TO DO, NOT FULL OF WHAT YOU THINK YOU SHOULD DO.**

I also stopped accepting so many meetings, and I put time limits on the ones I did accept. I had gotten in the habit of accepting too many meetings, then suffering through them while feeling anxious about all the work that I could be getting done if I weren't stuck in a meeting that was going on and on.

So anytime I was tempted to schedule a meeting with someone, I would first ask myself, "Why?" I discovered that when I asked myself why I needed to meet with the person, very often the issue the other person wanted to discuss could be handled by email or with a much shorter phone meeting.

I also learned to schedule my meetings not in increments of sixty minutes (because that looks so tidy on a calendar), but by how much time I thought the issue needed. There's a rule in time management that says, "The time it takes to complete any activity will expand to fill the time allotted on the calendar." Many meetings that could be done in ten minutes expanded to sixty because that's the time I had allotted on the calendar. After a month of being more aware of this, my meetings were cut down by over half.

2. Learn to say no to self and others

I also had to learn to say no to things I really enjoyed. I love watching funny YouTube videos and updating my Pinterest boards, but I could not give my time to them during the work week. Instead, I chose to do those things at night on the weekend. (And if you follow me on Pinterest, let me just apologize for sometimes clogging up your feed late at night on the weekends.)

Every decision we make about how to spend our time involves a trade-off. We can do this, not that. Go to this spot for vacation, not that. Spend an hour doing this, not that, and so on. It sounds simple, but when we become aware of this, we tend to spend our time on more worthwhile activities.

Writing this book, for example, is a trade-off for me. I spent my Saturdays writing. That means I've had the uncomfortable but good and necessary experience of saying no to lots of people over the last several months.

● ● ● ● ● ●
OUR GOALS IN DIFFER-ENT SEASONS OF OUR LIVES DETERMINE HOW WE SPEND OUR TIME.

"No, I'm sorry we can't go to a get-together." "No, I can't volunteer for this thing or that." "No, I can't go to the grocery store." (Okay, that one is for my husband, and seriously, who even wants to go to the grocery store anyway, am I right, ladies?)

My goal of writing this book changed how I chose to spend my time for a season of my life. Throughout our lives, our goals determine how we spend our time.

Friends who love you understand when you have seasons where you have to say no more often. Real friends support each other's dreams and lives. Do real friends get disappointed? Sure. But real friends always love each other even when disappointment happens.

You may be thinking, "Saying no sounds easy, Alli, but I hate disappointing people. It's harder than you make it sound." I get it, and I feel your pain. It's never fun or easy to disappoint people. You feel momentary discomfort no matter how good your reasons are for saying no.

During a keynote session at BlissDom one year, Brene Brown, speaker and author of *Daring Greatly*, said something that stuck with me: "Choose discomfort over resentment." Choose the momentary awkwardness of saying no (with love) and disappointing someone rather than saying yes and resenting it later.

How many times have you said yes to a commitment you knew you didn't want to do, you didn't have time to do, and you wouldn't enjoy doing? If you are like me, you said yes, told yourself you'd make it work somehow, and hated every minute of it.

Isn't it crazy that we find it easier to say yes to something that will make us miserable, than to say no, feel awkward for a few minutes, and go on living our happy lives? It makes no sense, but we all have a tendency to do it.

Setting boundaries in our lives is the only way to ensure we stay healthy physically, mentally, and spiritually. Jesus himself set boundaries around his time. One of my favorite stories is in Mark 4:35–40.

That day when evening came, he said to his disciples, "Let us go over to the other side." Leaving the crowd behind, they took him along, just as he was, in the boat. There were also other boats with him. A furious squall came up, and the waves broke over the boat, so that it was nearly swamped. Jesus was in the stern, sleeping on a cushion. The disciples woke him and said to him, "Teacher, don't you care if we drown?"

He got up, rebuked the wind and said to the waves, "Quiet! Be still!" Then the wind died down and it was completely calm.

He said to his disciples, "Why are you so afraid? Do you still have no faith?" [And for some reason, in my mind, he then groggily laid back down on his cushion and went back to sleep.]

Here's what is so great to me about this passage: Jesus sees that there is work to be done. He sees the crowd. He knows people need to be healed, demons need to be cast out, and lessons need to be taught. But he still tells his disciples to get in the boat, and once there, he falls asleep. Yes, the needs of the people are urgent, and their requests (or cries) for healing must have been compelling, but Jesus knows that he needs to stop and rest.

Learning to politely and kindly turn down requests can be tricky at first if you are not used to saying no. They don't call "people pleasing" a disease for nothing! Remember as you say no, you're not rejecting the individual, you're simply declining their request. This isn't personal, it's about you respecting your own time limitations.

What to Add In

When I made the decision to see where I spent my time, I discovered how many distractions I let clutter up my day. But even more significantly, I discovered what I *wasn't* making time for.

As my friend Christine often says to me, "You don't burn out doing the right things. You burn out because of what you don't do." We can say no to nonessentials in order to do lots of great things in our lives. We can work all day and all night doing what God calls us to do. But without adding *in* time to connect with him and others regularly, we will burn out even on good activities.

1. Add in time to stay connected to God through prayer and Scripture

One of the most beautiful reminders I have of the importance of spending intentional time with God is found in Matthew 14. John the Baptist has just been beheaded, and Jesus wants to be alone, so he retires to a private place to grieve. But the crowds hear that he is there and follow him. He has compassion on them and heals the sick among them. Then he performs the miracle of the feeding of the five thousand. And Scripture tells us this: "Immediately Jesus made the disciples get into the boat and go on ahead of him to the other side, while he dismissed the crowd. After he had dismissed them, he went up on a mountainside by himself to pray … alone."

Once again we see Jesus leave the crowd, with work still to be done, to take care of what is important. He knows he needs to connect to his Father, to pour out his heart to him, to rest in the comfort of his arms as he grieves the loss of John the Baptist. He doesn't rush around to fix everything for everyone. He could have — he is God, after all. But he is also a human being who needs to spend time alone with God.

We too must add into our lives what is important to the well-being of our souls.

I used to rush through my day and send up little "Help me, Jesus" prayers during my crazy day. Not only was I busier than a one-legged man in a butt-kicking contest, I never felt any peace at all.

WE MUST ADD INTO OUR LIVES WHAT IS IMPORTANT TO THE WELL-BEING OF OUR SOULS.

I'm a night owl, so I decided that I would pray at night. Guess what happened? Did I pray late at night? Nope. I never did. I played on my phone, texted with friends, and read ... but prayer? Nope. Not at night. That was when I could get a lot done, after all!

I knew I had to learn to become a morning person and get up to pray and have quiet time before the kids woke up and the hurricane of morning activity in the household started. So I began to wake up earlier every day to pray and read my Bible.

It still hurts when my alarm goes off so early, and I need two cups of coffee to get going, but when I stay connected to God and prioritize that time, I am more likely to spend the rest of my day focused on the important instead of the urgent. There's no right or wrong way to spend time alone with God each day. I remember in the early days of my faith, I heard that I should spend twenty minutes a day having a "quiet time" with the Lord. But later in life I met a woman who told me she never used the words "quiet time" to describe the time she spent connecting with God each day. Instead she calls it "unhurried time with the Lord." I love the picture that paints. It's not rushed, it's intentional, it's purposeful, and it's meaningful. Exactly what staying connected to God through prayer and Scripture should be like.

2. Add in time to connect with others

We have to be intentional about connecting with others, including our spouse, our children, and our friends. It's easy to allow our work, even our work for the Lord, to keep us from purposefully connecting with those we love.

Throughout the Gospels, we see that Jesus spent time with those he loved. He spent weeks on end traveling with his disciples. Sure, they did ministry together. They even performed miracles together. But Jesus also went to weddings. He visited his mother and brothers. He hung out with his great friend Lazarus and Lazarus's sisters, Mary and Martha. (Of course, he had to raise him from the dead first …) Jesus was a man who not only understood the importance of spending time with those he loved, he modeled it throughout his time on earth.

3. Add in time to take care of yourself

Breaking busy also means adding in space, time, and energy to take care of yourself. Just as you would make an appointment to go to the doctor, make appointments during the week to exercise, to read that book you have been putting off, to take a bubble bath, or even just to lie on your bed and stare at the ceiling.

You have permission to take care of you because the world needs what only you can bring to it. Your colleagues, your family, they need you to be who you were created to be, and you were not created to be overstressed and overbusy.

Are you doing things today that are urgent? Or important? When we put every choice through that filter, we are able to prioritize how to spend our time instead of being busy with no direction.

Action Steps

1. Try doing a time diary experiment for a week. Download a printable Breaking Busy diary at AlliWorthington.com/BreakingBusy.

2. What activities drain you and prevent you from reaching your goals in life? Make a stop-doing list and learn to say no.

3. What activities are important to you? Add them to your calendar.

4. Schedule in one hour next week to do something to take care of yourself. It can be reading a book, getting your hair done, getting a massage, whatever you have been putting off. Dr. Alli's orders!

EIGHT

DECISIONS

*Finding Your Confidence
in a World of Choices*

Hungry and ready to enjoy dinner, I settled in to a dimly lit, comfortable booth at the back of a steakhouse with my friends Christine and Nick. I read the entire menu, thought about the options carefully, and then decided on the salmon. (I do this at every restaurant: I review all the choices carefully and then always, and I mean always, choose the salmon. It's a fact that makes my husband, Mark, crazy, but after this many years of marriage, I guess he's used to it.)

My dinner dates, Christine and Nick Caine, are some of the most wonderful people I have come to call friends. They are the founders of The A21 Campaign, an organization that works to abolish human trafficking around the world. Years before at a leadership conference, I heard Chris preach for the first time and learned that over 27 million people today are enslaved in some way. I wanted to get up, stand on my chair, and holler because I admired her work so much. Chris and I were introduced socially in the winter of 2013, and I was happy to join the advisory group of the new women's initiative she was planning to build. Since joining her advisory group, I had been weighing in on her new project, Propel Women, and was looking forward to diving into more details over dinner. Propel Women is a women's organization that seeks to equip and empower women to lead others to Christ in whatever sphere of life they are in — leading their children in the playroom as a stay-at-home mom, leading a group of volunteers in the community, leading a company from a boardroom as a corporate CEO, and everything in between. Wherever God has placed women, women are called to lead others to him, as Christ followers.

Propel was just in the planning stages, and Christine was looking for someone to run all the day-to-day operations and work out her vision for the organization. Halfway through my salmon, after I made suggestions as to who would be a great candidate to help run Propel, Christine stopped me midsentence and said, "Alli, we want *you* to help us run Propel."

I almost choked on that bite of salmon. I was shocked.

Laughing out loud, I said, with all the manners I could muster, "Me? That is a terrible idea!"

Christine confidently replied, "No, it's you. You are who we need to help us run it."

"Nope, terrible idea," I said again, the confidence in my voice now matching that of hers.

I looked back and forth at their faces and felt dizzy. These were brilliant people sitting in front of me. Surely they could see this was not a good idea.

I insisted, "Absolutely not. I'm an entrepreneur. I build things. I've never even had a 'real' job. You do not want me!"

Chris didn't miss a beat. "Alli, we are doing something new. We're not pouring new wine into old wineskins. Propel needs someone who can create something that has never been done. A visionary, a risk taker. You are who we need to help us build this organization."

Because I am not as classy and well-spoken as I could be, I wiped my mouth with my napkin, placed it gently back in my lap, and said in a voice heavy with sarcasm, "Well, Chris, Jesus is going to have to clearly tell us both that I should do this, because I think it's a terrible idea."

Christine laughed and, in her wonderful Australian accent, said, "No, Jesus is just going to have to tell *you*."

Of course we both laughed at her pronouncement. Hers, the laugh of a woman confident in her decision, and mine, the laugh of a woman nervously hoping someone would change the subject.

As if predicting my objections to the job, Christine told me, "By the way. You and your husband have five sons and a life here. You wouldn't have to move your family. You can run the operations of Propel for us from Nashville. I don't care where you do it, but I do know you *can* do it."

I nodded along as Christine and Nick continued to talk excitedly about Propel. Sometimes I was just watching their lips move while I thought about how tough it was going to be to let them down when I told them no.

I never imagined saying yes.

After dinner, they walked me to my car. As I drove away, I glanced back at them, holding hands and walking down the city sidewalk back to their hotel. I knew with some time and distance they'd come to their senses, and I would be able to let them down easy.

On the drive home, with every traffic light I passed, I had more and more arguments in my head as to why I wouldn't take the job. I had been on my own as a consultant and coach for over a year and finally felt comfortable truly trusting that God had led me there.

In my head I heard:

"I'm an entrepreneur."

"I build companies. I don't work for other people."

"I'm a coach and consultant for businesses. I help people build companies. I'm not a 'job' person. No way."

"The last thing I am going to do is put my and my family's security and future in the hands of someone else. No way! Too risky!"

Even louder than my thoughts that I wasn't a job person was my battle with fear. Fear told me I couldn't do it, that I would let people down, that it was too big of a risk, and that I wasn't cut out for helping build and run a ministry. In short, I wasn't "good" enough. If only the decision were as cut and dried as steak versus salmon!

Analysis Paralysis

Making decisions can be one of the hardest things we do. When we have to make a choice, it's easy to get stuck because of fear that we might choose the wrong one. This "analysis paralysis" causes us to waste a lot of time and energy and keeps us busy rethinking our options and replaying our decisions.

Two factors typically come into play with analysis paralysis. We either (1) let fear tell us we will make the wrong decision and freeze, or (2) we refuse to refine our choices, become overwhelmed by the sheer scope of them, and shut down.

As a result, we waste time and energy when making even the most mundane decisions because we lack the confidence to make a decision in a world of options. But what if I told you it doesn't have to be that way? Because it doesn't. I'll show you how.

The Importance of Developing a Decision-Making Framework

Andy Stanley, pastor and author, sums up the impact of our daily decisions and actions this way:

> Direction — not intentions, hopes, dreams, prayers, beliefs, intellect, or education — determines destination. I know it's tempting to believe that our good intentions, aspirations, and dreams somehow have the ability to do an end run around the decisions that we make on a daily basis.... [However,] you and I will win or lose in life by the paths we choose.[20]

Like it or not, every single decision we make takes us down the road closer to the destination that is our future. What we think, believe, hope for, study, or dream about doesn't affect the outcome of our future. The decisions we make and the actions we take do. With that much depending on our decision-making ability, it's no wonder we become paralyzed. That's why having and using a decision-making framework is so important.

A decision-making framework is a systematic approach that allows us to filter our choices, narrow down our options, and confidently make a decision. By using the framework, we destroy analysis paralysis, ultimately saving the time and energy we would typically have spent frozen in fear or overwhelmed by options. I'm not saying that having a decision-making framework keeps you from that initial feeling of fear and of being overwhelmed, but it does move you quickly out of that stage and toward a good decision.

My Decision-Making Framework

I'd like to tell you that I developed my decision-making framework as a result of an incredible strategy session with a think tank of brilliant minds. But that's not what happened. I was talking with a coaching client about the need to narrow down options in our lives, and she asked how in the world I did that. In talking the issue out with her, I realized I did actually have a system, one I had refined over the years. I realized I made my decisions based on the most important things in my life: faith, family, future, fulfillment, and friends.

When I left my meeting with her, I knew I needed to do two things: I needed to write down my decision-making framework, and I needed to share it with others. The first place I shared it was in a business group that I coached, a group from many different faith backgrounds. The response was overwhelmingly positive. I guess I never realized how many people struggle to find confidence in a world of choices.

Many of the people in the group later commented that having a decision-making framework reduced the fear associated with making a "bad" decision and made them feel more confident in the decisions they made. So let's take a quick look at what I call "The Five Fs of Decision Making" and see how I applied them to my decision about Propel.

The Five Fs of Decision Making

1. Faith

In any decision in life, it is most important to pray and look for answers in Scripture. James 1:5 tells us, "If any of you lacks wisdom, you should ask God, who gives generously to all without finding fault, and it will be given to you." We have to trust that the God of the universe is working out something great in our lives. Knowing that, we have to continue to seek his wisdom and then stay the course.

Two mornings after I met with the Caines, I did the one thing that to me is the most important step of my decision-making framework: I actually prayed about it. (As I said, having a system doesn't keep you from initially feeling fear and of being overwhelmed, it just moves you out of it more quickly.) I knelt down beside my bed (because Jesus knows you're serious when you kneel, am I right?) and asked, "Lord, should I do this?" As clear as day, I sensed the answer. It was very simple: "Do it."

Huh?

Well, I was not expecting that.

In that moment, God's direction was very, very clear. That doesn't happen in every decision I make — in fact, it rarely does. That's why the first part of my framework is *faith*. It's not prayer. It's not read the Bible. It's not listen for God's voice to be crystal clear. It's a combination of all of those things, all the things that make up my faith. Yes, I pray. That's a big part of it. And yes, I hope that God's directions to me are as crystal clear as they were this time. And of course I read Scripture because I believe what it says in 2 Timothy 3:16–17: "All Scripture is God-breathed and is useful for teaching, rebuking, correcting and training in righteousness, so that the servant of God may be thoroughly equipped for every good work." (I'll be the first to admit that I never found a Scripture that says, "Alli, take that job and close your consulting company" or any other such directive. I wish. That would be so handy!)

But I do know that when I make a decision, it must be in line with the principles in Scripture and in line with my faith. As a

Christian organization, Propel fell in line with my faith. And God had confirmed in my spirit that I could do this. But I still needed to consult my husband, which leads me to the next "F" ...

2. Family

When making a decision, you have to ask, "How does this decision affect my family?" If you're married, what does your spouse say? Are you in agreement? I'll tell you, there have been many decisions in my life (including leaving BlissDom) where I prayed Mark would be my "no."

After I prayed about working with the Caines and felt God's leading, I took the topic to my husband, as I always do. I hadn't expected that I would hear God tell me to take the job, so I had never even mentioned the job offer to Mark. (I know, you'd think it would have come up in small talk, but it didn't. That's how sure I was that it wasn't going to happen!)

Once again, I sat him down on our couch in the living room, just as I had done two years earlier to tell him about my call to leave BlissDom.

"Hey, babe," I said. "I have something crazy to talk to you about."

Mark looked worried. "Uh oh. All right. Is it bad?" (He always likes to prepare himself, you know?)

"Nope, not bad, just kind of unexpected. God is moving and telling me to make another change, I think ..."

And with that I blurted out the whole story, the offer, the new wine in a new wineskin, the visionary, the risk-taker, and the goal of the new ministry.

Being the practical man he is, he asked only a few questions. "Who is Chris again?"

Chris is kind of like a female Pentecostal Billy Graham.

"Is she the real deal?"

Yes. Her heart is for Jesus.

"Do you believe in this organization?"

Yes.

"Do you feel confident you can do it well?"

Kind of. I mean, yeah. I can do it.

"We don't need to move to California?" (A factor that would have a *big* impact on our family.)

Nope.

"Do you want to do it?"

I think so.

"Did you pray about it?"

Yes.

"What did you hear?"

Do it.

"Well, tell Christine you are in."

And there it was. God was in and Mark was in, and you'd think that would be enough of a go-ahead for me to make the decision. But there were other factors I still wanted to consider if I was going to feel confident about the decision I needed to make. We were talking about our future here, and this decision could not be taken lightly.

3. Future

When evaluating a choice, it is important to think about the future you.

What is your goal in this situation? What do you hope to accomplish?

Does this decision seem to be leading you to who you want to become and how you want to grow as a person?

Whether this is a big goal or a little goal, a big decision or a little decision, looking at where you want to be as a result of your decision is critical for making the right choice.

I like to ask myself what "future Alli" will think about decisions. Whether it is eating that extra piece of carrot cake with ice cream (and I can put away extra pieces of carrot cake and ice cream!) or taking time away from writing this book and the family to speak at an event. When I think of what "future Alli" will be happy with, it makes the decision making clearer.

When I thought about working with Christine and Nick Caine and being the executive director of Propel Women, I asked myself, "Does this line up with my future work, life, and personal goals?" On every account, the answer was yes.

I wanted to be able to continue to provide for our family so Mark could continue to live out his present calling to be a daily hands-on influence in the lives of our five sons. Working with Propel allowed me to continue doing that.

I asked myself what "future Alli" thought of this decision and realized "future Alli" was all in as well. I could see myself in the future being happy that I took the risk and joined the vision. It seemed God and everyone else was on board with the decision for me to say yes to the Caines and yes to Propel Women.

But if I'm nothing else, I'm thorough. I knew my decision-making framework worked for me, and this was going to be one of the biggest decisions of my life, so you can bet your boots I was going to keep moving through my framework. I moved on to the next F: fulfillment.

4. Fulfillment

When making big decisions, it is crucial to ask yourself what makes you feel fulfilled. Your passions and talents give you a clue into what you were created to do, and they help you make sure you're not living life bound by the things you think you "should" do.

I love helping people, specifically women, identify their calling, build their skill sets, and reach their goals in life. Working with Propel would certainly allow me to continue doing that, and probably with a much broader scope.

In deciding whether to work with Propel Women, I had to lose the false belief that my identity was wrapped up in a specific consulting career, just as I had to learn my identity wasn't wrapped up in running BlissDom. My calling is to help women be successful in work and life. So once again, embracing life with an organization that was in line with what fulfills me seemed like a no-brainer. But I had one last step to go through before I finally decided.

5. Friends

When making big decisions, wise counsel from friends and mentors is always a good idea. This doesn't mean I post an update on Facebook and ask all my Facebook friends to weigh in on my most important decisions. The friends I'm talking about are people who have earned the right to speak into my life. By earned the right, I mean that they are trustworthy, they have my best interests at heart, and their own lives bear the fruit of wise decision making. Instead of trying to get feedback and opinions from lots of people, it's best to focus on three or four of the wisest friends we have and ask them for their thoughts on the matter. They are our wise counselors.

• • • • • •

DON'T ASK ALL YOUR FACEBOOK FRIENDS TO WEIGH IN ON YOUR MOST IMPORTANT DECISIONS. ASK THE FRIENDS WHO HAVE EARNED THE RIGHT TO SPEAK INTO YOUR LIFE.

Another principle I follow when it comes to asking my friends is this: Don't ask people who have a vested interest in your life. You can't ask your next-door neighbor if she thinks you should move. If you're a great neighbor, she'll say no. If you're a terrible neighbor, she'll say yes. Either way, she has a vested interest.

And you shouldn't seek counsel from people who could financially benefit from your decision. Money can so quickly and easily cloud our judgment, so it's always best to avoid asking the opinions of those who may profit from our good (or bad) decisions.

We'll dive more into the topic of friends and wise counselors in the next chapter on communication, but for now, let's just agree that decision making by a popularity vote is never a good idea. You want the opinion of others, just not the opinion of everyone in your contact list.

I was fairly certain I knew what I was going to do about working with the Caines, but I had a few valued and trusted friends I consulted first. They were people I knew were connected to Jesus daily, who would pray before they weighed in, who didn't have a vested interest one way or another in my decision. They were friends I could count on to tell me the truth. Every single one prayed and came back to me with their own version of "I think you should do it!"

The Decision

And with that, my life changed forever.

On Saturday morning, not knowing any real details about the job specifics, and in the most modern way, I accepted the job via text message. (Yes, you read that right. I texted my new boss to accept the job!)

I'm in. I very clearly confirmed that I'm supposed to do this with you. I will work on laying out details and send it to you on Monday. I'm thrilled and a wee bit nervous and overjoyed at the same time. Love you!

Christine replied,

About time you heard from God. ☺ I love you!

The Caines had no idea about all that I had done to make sure I was making a good decision. Their friendship and kindness, their belief in me, and their good work all over the world — all of those things could have easily swayed me to say yes to them. But I needed to be sure that yes was the right answer. It needed to be right with God, with my family, with my future, for my fulfillment, and with my friends whom I call my wise counsel.

I have never second-guessed that decision, even in the beginning when the work of building something new was a struggle and the travel took me far from home far too many days in a row. My framework served me well in this life-altering decision.

Smaller Decisions

Making decisions using a framework takes some practice. To get yourself in the habit of using the framework, you might want to practice using it on some of the smaller decisions in your life. Once you've gotten used to the framework, you can take the following shortcuts:

1. Choose the most relevant part of the framework

You don't have to make every decision with the whole five-step process. Use whichever points in the framework are appropriate for the decision to be made. I mean, every time Mark and I decide where we want to go to dinner, I'm not on my knees in my bedroom quizzing myself on the Five Fs. I'm sure Mark would leave me there with my fabulous framework and enjoy dinner without me!

2. Go for the quick 10-10-10 analysis

I don't always have the benefit of a lot of time to think about the future impact of a decision. When I don't, I rely on Suzy Welch's 10–10–10 process. In her book *10–10–10*, Welch teaches that the way to make decisions is to ask yourself how you will feel about your decision after 10 minutes, 10 months, and 10 years.[21] It's so simple and so brilliant, and I use it all the time.

For example, recently I was given the opportunity to speak at an event in New York. Like most decisions, it wasn't an easy one. It was a great event, and I knew I could speak on the topic of calling and faith and add to the event. But the time commitment was long, considering travel to and from the event, and as much as I wanted to go, I had to weigh the cost (time away from my family and work) with the benefits (I love speaking and it makes me happy to speak). After going to my framework, I realized that the family step of the framework outweighed all the possible good.

The 10–10–10 framework also helped. In this circumstance I would have felt great to say yes after the first 10 minutes. It always feels good in the moment to say yes and not go through the momentary discomfort of disappointing others. But after 10 months I would have completely regretted saying yes because I would be neck deep in editing this book, and my workload with Propel would be even greater. The offer that sounded great at first would have taken lots of time and energy, disrupting my life for an entire week (and maybe more).

After 10 years, I may or may not have regretted the decision. I probably wouldn't even remember it unless at the event I met my new best friend or if I missed a book deadline because of it.

The 10 minutes and 10 months questions, however, were enough to make me feel confident about declining the offer.

3. Turn the tables and get some distance

Take a minute and pretend that your best friend is coming to you for advice on making this same decision you are trying to make. What would your advice be? I once was at a conference where the speaker, Chip Heath, led the audience through how shockingly simple this tool is for making better decisions.

Here's how he explained it:

You are single and thinking of calling someone you are interested in from your psychology class. You like her, but you've only talked with her once. (Obviously, this was an event with mostly men in attendance.)

Option One: Wait until you talk to her more.

Option Two: Call her.

Now, switch it around. Same scenario, but your best friend wants your advice. What would you recommend? Most of the audience yelled out, "Call her." It was so simple when the advice was for someone else and not ourselves.

For me, this trick is the handiest when it comes to parenting decisions. I realize I'm sometimes too close to my kids to always make the best decision. I get swayed because I love them,

I believe only the best about them, and, well, I made them. I'm biased, and I can't pretend I'm not.

Recently our oldest son, Justin, tried to convince Mark and me that we should let him attend a New Year's Eve party hosted by his friend from church. (They always sucker us in with the church card!) He reminded us how responsible he is, how his friends had strong testimonies, and how their parents would be there. We wanted to say yes because we love him and believe the best about him (and his arguments were brilliant).

But when we stepped back and asked ourselves, "If this was the son of a close friend (who was equally wonderful and trustworthy), would we advise that they let him stay out past midnight?"

Of course not!

We could have listed ten reasons why it wasn't a good choice to let him stay out past midnight on New Year's Eve, and when we put anyone but our kid in the position, it was an easy no. Yet when it came to our own kid, with all our love and biases, we were wringing our hands trying to decide what would be best.

Justin didn't get to stay out on New Year's Eve, needless to say. Was he disappointed? Yes. Did he get over it quickly? You bet.

I would never advise my best friend to make a bad decision, and by turning the tables, I can remove some of the emotional baggage of making the decision for myself. The Heath brothers in their book *Decisive* call this phenomenon "social distance."[22]

So when you have a decision to make, just ask yourself, "What would I tell my best friend to do?"

Wholly Lean on Jesus' Name

It's easy to overthink every decision we make. Every day we face an avalanche of decisions, from the minor to the major. Even when we have a great framework for making those decisions, we still wonder if we are making the right decision for ourselves, for our family, and for our future. In those moments, I remind myself of the truth found in Philippians 4:6–7:

> Do not be anxious about anything, but in every situation, by prayer and petition, with thanksgiving, present your requests to God. And the peace of God, which transcends all understanding, will guard your hearts and your minds in Christ Jesus.

It's like the words to an old familiar hymn:

> My hope is built on nothing less
> than Jesus' blood and righteousness
> I dare not trust the sweetest frame,
> but wholly lean on Jesus' name.[23]

Yes, finding my confidence in a world of choices requires a framework for good decision making. But I "dare not trust the sweetest frame." (And I think my framework is pretty sweet!) Good decision making requires me to remember and lean on the One whom I have placed my confidence in in the first place.

Action Steps

1. Download your copy of the decision-making framework at AlliWorthington.com/BreakingBusy.

2. Apply the framework (or just one part of it) to a decision you are currently facing, whether it's a big or small decision.

3. Use the 10–10–10 framework on a decision you are facing.

4. Ask your future self what she thinks of the decision you are making.

NINE

COMMUNICATION

Finding Your Voice in a World of Noise

I love movies. I love going to the theater, I love the popcorn, I love the giant drinks, and I even love sneaking in candy in my purse so I don't have to spend $25 for candy for all the boys. (Don't tell anyone!) When a new Disney movie is released in theaters, you can be sure the boys and I will be there on opening day.

Mark, on the other hand, loved going to movies with me when we were dating, then after we got married announced, "Now that we aren't dating anymore, can we just start renting them? I like to watch them at home. You too?"

I was appalled. I love the giant screen, the too-loud speakers, and even the sticky seats (Can we all give an amen to whoever invented hand sanitizer?). I am in it for the experience! We laughed at his bait and switch, and I've been going to movies with girlfriends, and now with our sons, ever since.

When I'm in the mood to see something heavy, I call my friend Shannon. Shannon is very artsy, very sophisticated, and a riot to be around, so a movie date with her is always a great time. Funny thing is, though, for two years I absolutely hated going to the movies with Shannon.

When Shannon and I first met a few years ago, I nodded in

agreement when she told me how much she loved dark, awful movies. But I regretted it, because I hate movies with dark topics with the heat of a thousand suns. But she loved them, and I wanted her to love me, so I pretended to love them too.

After two years of trips to the movies with my friend, I had finally had enough. I decided I was ready to come clean. The very next week, I met Shannon for coffee with my well-practiced, well-prepared talking points in my head. My plan was to go back to the beginning of our friendship and explain I wanted to learn to like the movies she loved, and I didn't mean to be dishonest, but I had been and now I was wasting too many hours of my life watching movies I hated.

However, instead of my well-rehearsed talking points, I, in typical Alli style, blurted it all out. I expected her to be hurt. Hurt because I lied, hurt because I didn't really like what she liked, and, most importantly, disappointed in me. She wasn't any of those things. All she did was laugh. She had figured out long ago that I didn't share her love of dark movies, but she didn't know how to bring it up without possibly hurting my feelings. (I guess those heavy sighs and frequent trips to the ladies room were a dead giveaway! And all that time I thought I was being so sneaky!)

• • • • • •
SOMETIMES WE WANT PEOPLE TO LOVE US, SO WE SILENCE OUR VOICE.

Now Shannon will text me selfies in front of movie posters when she's about to go see some horribly depressing movie, and I send her selfies in front of great feel-good movies I'm about to see. When we do go to a movie together, it's something we both know we'll love!

And here's the thing, we would both still be spending our precious free time awkwardly seeing movies together had I not decided to finally find my voice and communicate honestly with her. We were so busy trying not to disappoint one another that we were actually disappointed *by* one another. What a colossal waste of time and emotional energy for both of us.

I'm sure you can identify. Too often our inability to communicate well causes us to become busy doing unnecessary things.

How Does Good Communication Help Us Break Busy?

Developing good communication skills might seem like a strange way to break busy. But ask yourself these questions:

- How much time have you wasted in office gossip that only made you feel more anxious and insecure?
- How much time have you lost on fruitless arguments with your teenager?
- How much time have you spent wishing your husband or friend or boss understood you?
- How much time have you lost chatting on the phone when you were trying to say good-bye and hang up?
- How much time have you frittered away with people who talk too much but are completely unaware of it (or worse yet, maybe *you* are the one who talks too much)?

Taking a good look at how we communicate and why, how others communicate, and how our fast-paced world *wants* us to communicate is an important part of cutting out busyness from our lives.

Identify Your Own Communication Style

I have come to the conclusion that there are three primary types of communication styles in this world. There are the over-communicators, the undercommunicators, and those who fall right smack in the middle of the two (the Goldilocks "just right" communicators).

Overcommunicators

Overcommunicators love to talk. So in terms of communication, that's a bonus, right? No wasting time having to constantly go back for more information. These people have it covered. Overcommunicators are thorough and love to make sure they are getting their points across ... their points and all the details that back up all their points ... and all the subtle nuances in between.

The danger in being an overcommunicator is that overcommunicators tend to waste time explaining unnecessary details or dominating conversations in such a way that they overwhelm those involved in the conversation. They overcommunicate when they are talking, emailing, sometimes even just updating their Facebook status (hello, too much information)! This can lead to others tuning out or skimming emails and other written correspondence and not getting the whole message.

• • • • • •

OVERCOMMUNICATORS ARE JUST TRYING TO MAKE SURE THEY ARE GETTING INFORMATION TO OTHERS, BUT INFORMATION OVERLOAD CAN CAUSE OTHERS TO TUNE THEM OUT.

In personal relationships, someone's natural tendency to overcommunicate can be overwhelming. I have a couple friends who are over-askers. They ask me so many questions that I have even said, "I think you have exceeded your question-asking quota today." We've laughed about it, but it's true. Their most common way of over-asking is by text. One will send me a text, "How are you doing today?" And I'll think, "Oh, that's sweet. She's checking in with me. That's what good friends do. I love that about her."

So I'll text back, "Great. Busy, but great." (Isn't that everyone's answer these days? Via text, "busy" is code for "I can't talk right now.")

A few seconds will go by and she'll text. "Busy? What are you busy doing?"

I'll text something simple, "Work" or "Boy's activities."

It's texting. Your answers are supposed to be short and to the point!

She'll immediately text me back, "Work? That's so great. What are you working on?"

I'm not kidding when I tell you she will ask me twenty questions before she's done. The longer it goes on and the more my phone beeps, the more I can feel my frustration level rising.

The funny thing about my girlfriends who are over-askers is they are equally as frustrated with me because they want to have a conversation, and I'm giving them quick one- and two-word answers.

I have learned with these friends that the best way to save us time is to pick up the phone and call. Our thirty minutes of somewhat frustrating texting can be a fun phone call that lasts only five or ten minutes!

In business relationships, overcommunicators can hijack meetings, take us down rabbit trails in conversation, send out lengthy emails, and tell us long stories at the water cooler, all of which can be big time consumers. With my team at Propel, I encourage everyone to email things only when there are specific action items that need to be taken care of. Updates and backstories are better left to meetings. (Here's a tip for keeping overcommunicators in check in a meeting: Have an agenda, and when the overcommunicator begins overtalking, simply point out that you have a lot to get through on your agenda and you need to keep moving. It works like a charm!)

You might be an overcommunicator if you

- are always thinking of the next thing you want to say in a conversation.
- say good-bye several times in one phone call.
- have people walk away from you while you are talking.
- tend to lecture your children for lengthy periods of time, repeating the same thing over and over.
- have been accused of hijacking a business meeting.
- have had people tell you they skimmed your email and then ask you to "give them the bullets."

If you are an overcommunicator, here are some quick tips to help you overcome your desire to overcommunicate.

- Be a good listener. Consciously try to listen more than you speak. (I struggle with this one!) God gave us two ears and one mouth for a reason!
- Practice the art of the short good-bye. When ending a phone conversation, say good-bye at the end of the conversation and then hang up. People who overcommunicate tend to say good-bye multiple times before actually ending the conversation.
- Use short sentences in your emails and let your subject line keep you on target. If you have to write a longer email, use headings and bullet points so when people skim (and they will), they won't miss the most important points of your email.

- Understand and abide by the proper practices of social media, texting, and other modern forms of communication. (I'll cover that below.)

Undercommunicators

People who tend to talk less or hold back from expressing their true opinions or feelings are referred to as undercommunicators. Those who fall in this category rarely know this about themselves because it's not like anyone ever says, "Girl, you know what I wish about you? I just wish you talked more!" In a world filled with overcommunicators, it's easy for undercommunicators to stay under the radar.

But believe it or not, undercommunicators can waste just as much time and energy as their overly talkative counterparts. Undercommunication typically happens because people believe others already understand what they are saying (no need to clutter up the airwaves with unnecessary details or points of clarification), or they fear the confrontation or discomfort that may come from speaking up when they object or disagree with something or someone.

I have a friend who says, "In the absence of information, people will supply their own details." I think that quote perfectly sums up the problem with undercommunicators.

In the absence of information, people make stuff up, they make assumptions, they insert details that may not be accurate. Whether it is in a personal setting or a business setting, the lack of information and the subsequently inserted (and often *wrong*) information keep us going in circles, chasing busy like a dog chasing his tail in a windstorm.

A great example is texting with my undercommunicating husband, Mark. Here's an example of a texting scenario with him. Mark will send me a text message.

Mark: "When does your flight land exactly?"

Me: "What's with the tone? Is everything okay?"

Mark: "Yeah. Why?"

Me: "When does your flight land EXACTLY? Seems like you're mad about something."

Mark: "Babe, I'm just trying to plan dinner."

Me: "Okay, but you still sound mad. Can you throw in a smiley face or something?"

Mark: ☺

So now when Mark asks, "When does your flight land exactly?" I have learned to clarify, "You mean 'When does your flight land exactly because I'm planning dinner around when you'll be home?' or 'When does your flight land because I'm looking forward to seeing you?'"

His usual reply?

"Both."

That man. He's not good at texting, and he won't touch an emoji unless I force him, but I love him anyway. ☺

At work, undercommunication is one of the biggest reasons I've seen for stress and for wasted time and energy. I've seen this with bosses as well as employees. For example, I once had an assistant who would leave a meeting without a clear understanding of who was responsible for what action steps. But out of worry that I might think she wasn't great at her job, she wouldn't ask any clarifying questions. And because I was an undercommunicator and halfway expected her to read my mind, I didn't confirm we were all on the same page. We wasted a lot of time going back and forth in order to collect details and get the job done. (A great tip for working with undercommunicators is to follow up all conversations and meetings with a quick email outlining what was said, what is needed, and who is responsible, just to make sure you're all on the same page.)

I think a lot of undercommunication happens when we don't feel comfortable or courageous enough to say things people may not like. For example, had I simply told Shannon my movie preferences on our first lunch date, I would have saved myself the agony and wasted time of watching all those dark movies.

> • • • • • •
> **UNDERCOMMUNICATION OCCURS WHEN WE DON'T FEEL COMFORTABLE OR COURAGEOUS ENOUGH TO SAY THINGS PEOPLE MAY NOT LIKE.**

You might be an under-communicator if

- people are always asking you, "What did you mean by that?"
- you think people don't follow your directions well.
- people often fail to live up to your expectations.
- you have been accused of not caring enough to give your opinion.
- you find yourself doing things you don't want to do because you don't want to speak up.
- you are constantly frustrated because your children don't live up to your expectations and seem clueless as to what you have asked them to do.
- your spouse often complains, "I'm not a mind reader you know!"

If you are an undercommunicator, here are some quick, easy tips to help you overcome your tendency to say too little.

- Ask people to confirm they heard your directions clearly by repeating them back to you. (This is especially helpful with your kids.)
- Be willing to risk discomfort by speaking up when you disagree or have a differing opinion.
- Understand and abide by the proper practices of social media, texting, and other modern forms of communication. (I'll cover that below.)
- If you have a child who is an undercommunicator, when they sit down for homework, ask THEN if they have any projects coming up, permission slips they need signed, and so on. They might not always remember on their own, but some casual opportunities to talk about it might help!

Why We Sometimes Don't Communicate Well

Whether we are overcommunicators or undercommunicators, it's helpful to be aware of *why* we communicate the way we do.

1. We grew up with poor communication patterns

Some of us learned how to be poor communicators from the homes where we grew up. Breaking these patterns can take a lot of work later in life.

For example, I have a good friend who grew up in a home where they had to pretend everything was perfect. Her dad was an alcoholic, and her mom worked hard to keep the family "temperature" calm, cool, and collected. Bad feelings weren't allowed. If you had them, you kept them to yourself. If you disagreed with anyone, you disagreed in your head, never aloud. Outside of the other obvious problems this created for her in dealing with others, she never learned to communicate well. She was a classic undercommunicator, always afraid of rocking the boat and constantly having to find a roundabout way to express her needs.

After just a few months of being her friend (and business colleague), I could see that she often held back saying things that needed to be said. Her undercommunication wasted everyone's time, including hers, because she constantly had to clarify later on what she wanted or needed. Over time, I was able to encourage her to take the risk and communicate.

Another friend grew up in a home with eleven siblings and often felt as if she didn't have a voice. Now, as an adult, she has a tendency to repeat herself over and over (classic overcommunicator), unconsciously looking for validation.

Sometimes we have to forgive our families for being bad communicators and break busy by learning better communication patterns.

2. We think the other person should be able to read our minds

Mark and I often laugh about my desire for him to read my mind. (Well, truth be told, we didn't always laugh about it. But through the years, we've come to understand it's just one of the ways we are different.) When we were first married, I used to cause lots of unnecessary drama with my need for him to read my mind. I would notice that the trash needed to be taken out, and instead of just asking him to take out the trash, I'd think to myself, "I sure hope he notices the trash needs to be taken out." (Classic undercommunication move.) Later on, when the trash was still in the can, I would get frustrated because he didn't take it out. From there, I would escalate to feeling ignored (even though I never asked him to do it), and then somehow make the leap from feeling ignored to "You must not care because you don't ever do what I want!" (Okay, it's funny here, but you know in real life how that goes!)

I think we sometimes equate someone not knowing what we are thinking or feeling to them not caring for us. That simply isn't true. Now, on any given day, Mark can have a hundred different things coming his way (or more, considering that we have five rambunctious boys in the house)! Between after-school activities, homework, my business meetings, appliance breakdowns, meals, pets, vets, teacher conferences, doctor visits, vacation plans, and the other nine million pieces of information he is processing, it is quite possible that he can both love me *and* not know what I am thinking or feeling.

● ● ● ● ● ●
LOVING SOMEONE WITH ALL YOUR HEART STILL WON'T GIVE YOU MIND-READING POWERS.

The fact is, people can't read our minds. They don't know what we are thinking or feeling (okay, sometimes they do 'cause it's obvious!), and it just isn't productive or beneficial to think they do know. Instead of hoping someone knows what you want, and instead of waiting for them to ask you what you think or how you feel, take the initiative to communicate clearly what you are thinking and feeling. You'll be relieved at how much time and emotional energy it saves.

Talk about breaking busy!

3. We think "venting" is healthy communication

Too often we confuse being honest and sharing our feelings in a healthy way with ranting, being critical, and complaining. Even more often, "sharing of feelings" comes in the way of gossip. I'll confess to you, gossiping has been a problem for me in my life, something I had to seriously learn to shut down. I have shared gossip in the form of prayer requests (true story, and sad to admit), and I have also used the excuse of saying, "I'm just venting." It took me years to realize that venting only leads to more venting, gossip only leads to more gossip, and all that useless talk results in hurt feelings, damaged relationships, and lost time.

In Ephesians 4:29, Paul says, "Do not let any unwholesome talk come out of your mouths, but only what is helpful for building others up according to their needs, that it may benefit those who listen."

Venting and gossiping don't build up anyone, not the person speaking or the person who has the unfortunate spot of listening. That kind of talk is also a huge time waster for everyone involved.

Vent to God — he can handle your anger, your frustration, and your anxiety. Even "gossip" to God, telling him your thoughts or questions about someone else. Prayer is one of the best ways to grow in love for others.

When someone wants to gossip or vent to me, I have learned to say as gently as possible, "I'm sorry, but I'm not sure I'm the right person for you to be sharing this with. Have you talked to [other person's name] about all of this?" That usually shuts the conversation right down and saves both of us a lot of time (and energy).

Recognizing why we don't communicate well is a great first step to learning ways to communicate better in our day-to-day lives. The better we communicate, the less time we waste and the more time we have for the things we love.

Breaking Busy with Better Communication

Learning to communicate with people in their chosen form of communication can be one of the quickest ways to break busy. One friend often texts me because I am a texter (and she knows that about me), but she's a talker, not a texter. So texting with her was a time waster because what she really wanted to do was talk.

So let's take a quick look at the different forms of communication and how and when to use them to help us break busy. I'll take them in the order of most intimate to least intimate. When choosing one of these methods to communicate, you'll need to consider (1) the audience, (2) the sensitivity of the message, and (3) the time needed on both the sending and receiving ends for the message to be conveyed properly.

Face-to-face

In person is always the quickest, clearest, and most intimate way to communicate with someone, and it is the best method to use when the message is more sensitive. When we are face-to-face, we have the benefit of using nonverbal cues and emotions to clarify what we are trying to communicate.

If I have a smile on my face and am relaxed when I tell a friend, "Sure, go to lunch without me. I'm on a deadline. Have fun," she will know I really mean it because she can see it on my face and see how my body language reflects it. If I said it with a smirk and my arms crossed over my chest, she would immediately know I didn't really mean it.

But imagine reading in a text or email, "Sure, go to lunch without me. I'm on a deadline. Have fun." Communicating in writing can open up a Pandora's box of "Did she really mean that?" "Is she upset?" "Should I call her and check on her?"

In-person communication protects us from the needless back-and-forth of miscommunication.

Anytime you have something important to discuss, whether with a colleague, friend, or spouse, it's best to do it face-to-face to avoid any miscommunication that will cause everyone to waste time and energy.

Phone

When you can't manage to meet with someone in person and the message is more intimate or involved, pick up that phone.

When the conversation is important and there's any risk of your intention or emotion being misunderstood, don't rely on the written word. Or if it would take more time to go back and forth by emailing, use the phone. But if your message is more practical than emotional and it isn't complex, you can move on to the next less-intimate methods of communication.

Email

Oh, email. It's our blessing and our curse, isn't it? We can't live with it most days (How many times have you said, "My inbox is out of control"? Me too!), and we definitely can't live without it. Email allows us to have multiple conversations at one time, any time of the day. But with the speed and ease of communication also comes the added danger of being misunderstood.

It's important to keep two things in mind with your email communications:

1. Keep it as brief as possible. If you have a lot to say, schedule a phone call or plan to meet in person.
2. Add in emotional identifiers. Because it is so easy to be misunderstood when communicating with words only, it

is crucial to add in little cues for the reader as to how you mean the words you write. For me, even with work email, I add emoticons to some messages to make it crystal clear that I am happy or that the emotion behind what I'm saying is light and friendly.

And never, I mean never, deliver bad news via email. If you can't meet in person, pick up the phone. The person you are telling the bad news to will want to connect anyway, so why write out the email first? Just save time and energy and hop on the phone.

Texting

I love texting for keeping up with friends and family. A quick text to a friend to say hello, to share a picture, or even to tell them you are grateful for them is a great way to stay connected with those we love.

As with email, any type of text-based communication needs extra attention to emotions. I think this is why emojis are so popular. Emojis are one of the best things that have happened to communication in ages. Don't laugh, stay with me. Let me explain. Think about how to read and receive the message in each of these texts:

Sure, go to lunch without me. I'm on a deadline. Have fun.
🙂 🙂 😎

Sure, go to lunch without me. I'm on a deadline. Have fun.
🙁 😩 🙁

Sure, go to lunch without me. I'm on a deadline. Have fun.
😣 😫 😖

Now see how easy that was? With happy emojis, sad emojis, and angry emojis, you knew how it was meant. You had the emotional identifiers. With no emojis, you have no clue how to take it, right? Don't fear the emojis; they are silly, but they will save you and everyone you communicate with in text lots of time and energy. Yes, emojis will help you break busy.

😊 😃 😉 😎 😕 😠 😦 😣 😧 😖

Facebook and Twitter

No chapter on communication methods in a book titled *Breaking Busy* would be complete without addressing social networking, because social networking can be a huge time waster. I know this for a fact because I use an app on my computer called Rescue Time that tells me exactly how productive I am and exactly how much time I am wasting. It also tells me the number of hours I am on social media each week. When I first started using Rescue Time, I was shocked. The number of hours I spent on Facebook and Twitter alone was unreal, and that didn't include other apps like Instagram, Snapchat, or WhatsApp.

I quickly learned I needed to break busy by setting some hard-and-fast guidelines for communicating via social media.

1. During the day I use the "get in, get out" method. I log in, post a status, a tweet, or a photo, answer any messages I might have, and log out. I do this for every single type of social media network. (I let myself scroll through and check in on friends via social media on evenings and weekends.)
2. I do not conduct "business" by social media. If someone asks me a question via private message that is business related, I often reply, "Hey, do you mind sending this

question/discussion to me via email? I like to keep all my important conversations in one place."

3. If I am mad, sad, or anxious, I do not let myself update any social media platforms. I pray or talk to trusted friends and family, but I never, I mean *never*, let myself go vent on the Internet. Soon I will feel better, but that crazy, attention-seeking update will still be there for the world to see and scratch their heads, wondering if I'm okay or not. I've had an onslaught of private message of "Are you okay?" after I've posted something like this, and there are always hours of "Oh, yes, I'm fine. I was in a bad mood. Promise, I'm great!" replies that have to be sent. Talk about unnecessary complication and busyness in life!

Finally, here's a great tip I learned about communicating with others that works both personally and professionally. Want to know someone's chosen form of communication? Call them.

- If they don't answer, leave a voicemail. If they call you back, they are phoners.
- If they text you back, they are texters.
- If they email you back, they are emailers.
- Or send someone an email and ask a simple question.
- If they text you the answer, they are texters.
- If they call you back, they are phone people, and if they email you back, they are likely emailers!

Of course, you can't deal with every issue through someone else's preferred method of communication, nor can you always use your own preferred method. (Much as I hate it, I have to use the phone sometimes!) But staying alert to preferences helps because usually a person's preferred method is the one that is most efficient for them (and therefore most efficient for you when you communicate with them).

Managing the Communication of Others

When I was a young girl, we had a big ancient phone in our home. It hung proudly in our kitchen with the longest, most tangled cord you have ever seen in your life. As a little girl, the phone was off-limits to me as I couldn't reach it, and I had no idea of the proper etiquette necessary to answer the phone (and phone calls weren't going to be for me anyway). As a teenager, when phone calls were most likely *only* going to be for me, some pretty strict rules went with that phone privilege.

First and foremost was the time of day my friends were (and were not) allowed to call me. Next was how long I was allowed to be on the phone. We didn't have call waiting, so being on the phone all the time was not an option. We didn't talk on the phone during dinner, we didn't stay up all night on the phone, and when we finally got a cordless phone, we didn't carry the thing around with us all the time.

Then came cell phones, followed quickly by all of the other forms of modern-day communication. But social networking, texting, and phones, all designed to allow us to communicate more freely with one another, have become anything but freeing. People believe they have constant access to us, blurring all sense of appropriate boundaries, and creating a sense of busyness in our lives to which most of us have succumbed.

The pull of the electronic tether on our lives is strong and has done more to hurt communication, real honest-to-goodness communication, than I think most of us realize. When it comes to managing the communication of others through modern-day conveniences, we must break busy by setting firm boundaries, much like the phone rules my parents set for me during my teens. I try to do that by:

- Setting the do-not-disturb function on my phone. (With the iPhone, only calls from friends or family members in your Favorites will ring through when you have Do Not Disturb activated. It's great for parents of teens especially; we always need to be available for them when they are out in the world. Have mercy!)
- Using social media only as a way of casually chatting with friends and family. I never use it for important messaging or necessary conversations. (And I make sure my friends, family, and business colleagues understand that as well.)
- Guarding family time. At the end of my workday, emails, work-related text messages, and phone calls stop and my family gets my time. I try to stay off my phone during meals, family movie night, and other family time. (Though my boys will all tell you they have caught me texting a time or two. I'm a work in progress.)

It's crazy to think that something as simple as communicating better can help us break busy and find our voice in a world of noise, but it can and it does. Taking control of the multitude of ways you can communicate with others can literally give you hours back in your day.

Action Steps

1. Assess your communication style. Do you tend to overcommunicate or undercommunicate, or are you Goldilocks in between?

2. Identify one communication problem you have. Write it down and start taking small steps in your daily life to communicate more effectively. Sometimes just being aware of it makes all the difference.

3. Identify your favorite method of communication (phone, email, texting, Facebook). Then identify the preferred method of your colleagues and loved ones. When possible, use their preferred method.

4. Don't let that phone be the boss of you. Set rules for yourself (it's helpful to write them down) on how you will use electronic communication (phone, email, social media, texting, and messaging apps).

TEN

WORTH

*Finding Your Value in a World
of Never Good Enough*

I'll confess to you, I wanted to start this book with this chapter because it carries so much weight in our busy lives. But I thought, "There's no way I can start a book about how to find peace and purpose in a world of crazy with a chapter on shame." But the truth of the matter is, the lie of shame is often the reason we find ourselves living busy lives outside our calling. Let me explain.

The Lie of Shame

"Adam and his wife were both naked, and they felt no shame" (Genesis 2:25).

I always thought it strange that the writer of Genesis thought it important to say Adam and Eve were naked *and* unashamed, like some commentary on the human body or modesty. But now I realize that the word *shame* wasn't just carelessly tossed in there to round out the sentence. It is a key part of our fallen human condition.

Think about it this way:

- Prior to eating the forbidden fruit, Adam and Eve felt no shame in themselves.
- Their *first* action after sinning was to cover and hide themselves from each other because of their sudden shamefulness.
- Their *second* action was to hide themselves from God because they feared God would see and expose their shamefulness. "I heard you in the garden, and I was afraid because I was naked; so I hid" (Genesis 3:10).

As soon as Adam and Eve messed up, the Enemy started speaking shame over them, and he's been doing it ever since then.

Guilt, that sense of conviction that comes over us when we do something wrong, is healthy and moves us toward positive change. Shame, however, drives us into a never-ending cycle of trying to fix ourselves, to prove to the world and ourselves that we are not inherently flawed, that we have value.

The lie the Devil wants me to believe, and you to believe, is that we are never going to live beyond the consequences of our actions. It's a lie he's been perfecting since the beginning of time. But I'm here to tell you his lie, the shame he pours into us, serves one purpose: to distract us and keep us busy trying to prove to the world that we are perfect.

● ● ● ● ● ●

THE LIE OF SHAME SERVES ONE PURPOSE: TO DISTRACT US AND KEEP US BUSY TRYING TO PROVE TO THE WORLD THAT WE ARE PERFECT.

The lie tells us we will never be good enough, regardless of what we do with our lives or how we live out our calling.

On the flip side of the lie of shame is the lie of pride. If the Enemy can't make us doubt our worth, he makes us believe in an equally false version of it, one that tells us we are valuable because of our incredible efforts, sometimes even our efforts on behalf of God. But whether we believe the lie of shame or the lie of pride, each is rooted in our need to feel worthy.

Finding Our Worth

The key to having a healthy understanding of our worth is knowing to whom we belong. There have been library rows full of books written about worth. But without an understanding of God through a relationship with Jesus that is empowered by the Holy Spirit, we will never really understand the true source of our value.

> **KEEPING US BUSY TRYING TO PROVE OUR WORTH IS THE EASIEST WAY TO KEEP US FROM THE LIFE GOD CREATED US TO LIVE.**

Keeping us busy trying to prove our worth is the easiest way to keep us from the life God created us to live because it makes us think that our worth is based on what we do, instead of who God is.

Spending our lives being busy trying to prove our worth is how the Enemy fulfills the warning we read in John 10:10: "The thief comes only to steal and kill and destroy." But this verse does not just warn us of the Enemy's plan, it also reveals God's plan: "I have come that [you] may have life, and have it to the full." (Whenever I read this verse I say, "Because I have come, you, Alli, have great worth." Try adding your name and speaking that over yourself.)

The Lie of Not Enough

Not that long ago, I was having lunch with a woman I was mentoring who wanted to start her own side business teaching photography classes. She was a world-class photographer and had that patient, gracious spirit that great teachers have. As we waited for our food to arrive, I asked her what was holding her back, and she admitted, "Alli, I'm afraid." It was odd to me that she said "afraid" because truthfully, she's one of the coolest women I know. She had built her photography business from the ground up, and it was thriving. When I asked her what she was afraid of she said, "Pick a number! I'm afraid I'm not smart enough. I'm afraid I can't teach well enough. I'm afraid I'm not good enough."

I said, "In every sentence you just spoke you said, 'I am not enough — can't teach well enough, not smart enough, not good enough.' You are a Christian. Does that sound like the voice of God to you? Would he tell you that you aren't enough?"

She shook her head no and said, "I'm just afraid I am a fraud, that I will be a teaching disgrace, and that I'm totally unworthy of teaching anyone anything."

Looking her straight in the eye, like I do with my boys when they need to pay attention, I said, "What you are hearing is the voice of shame, and you are so shackled to that shame, you can't take one step forward to do what you were created to do. You are not a disgrace, because you serve a God who is grace-filled, and it is *that God* who makes you worthy."

● ● ● ● ● ●
WHEN YOU SERVE A GOD WHO IS GRACE-FILLED, IT IS *GOD* WHO MAKES YOU WORTHY.

Every day the Enemy lies to people, trying to distract them from their calling.

- He tells pastors they aren't worthy of teaching the Bible because they aren't perfect.
- He tells mothers they are doing a horrible job and their kids will suffer for their mistakes.
- He tells men they have to be at the top of the corporate ladder making six-figure salaries, even if it means never seeing their families.
- He tells teenagers that their parents' faith is meaningless and to abandon it if they want to really experience the life they are meant to live.

And he most likely tells you a lie that you believe.

But God reminds us that he offers us life — a rich, full, abundant life — free from striving for our own sense of perfection, a life resting in the assurance that we are already perfect because of the work he has done on the cross.

Authentic Worth

Jesus' redemptive love, his saving grace, and his forgiveness are what make us worthy. Our worth does not come through our great accomplishments, nor does it come from other people's acceptance (or rejection) of us. Jesus teaches us that our worth is in *him*. We are made in his image, crafted beautifully in the womb, full of passions and giftings, and with the potential to do amazing things through his power.

We must simply grasp that we are fearfully and wonderfully made. When we know our worth — and the glory from where it originates — we are able to break the cycle of busy that causes us to strive to prove (to ourselves and others) that we have value.

Fighting the Battle of Unworthiness

Much of the busyness we subject ourselves to comes from our desire to feel better about ourselves, to feel like we matter, to feel we have worth. We strive to buy that beautiful house, to have the perfect Facebook picture, to be the best classroom mom, and then we realize our new achievement doesn't make us any happier or more fulfilled than we were before.

• • • • • •

MUCH OF THE BUSYNESS WE HAVE IN LIFE IS BECAUSE WE ARE ALWAYS STRIVING TO FEEL BETTER, TO FEEL LIKE WE MATTER, TO FEEL WE HAVE WORTH.

When we live life feeling unworthy, we wonder if we will *ever* be enough — smart enough, creative enough, thin enough, rich enough, spiritual enough. We stay stuck in cycles of busyness trying to please others to gain assurance and acceptance. We overcommit, we say yes to things we don't want to do in the first place, we sign up for Bible studies we don't want to attend. (I even know of a couple who started the process to adopt children, not because they felt called to adoption, but because they thought that's what good Christians were supposed to do.) We repeat fruitless behaviors over and over again because we think if we just try "hard enough" next time, we'll get it right. But our striving to please only leads to more emptiness and frustration.

Fighting the battle of unworthiness is constant. The Enemy of this world is persistent, and because of that, we must always be battle ready or we will be battle weary.

One of the greatest chapters in all of the Bible (I say that about every book, chapter, and verse I love!) is Ephesians 6, Paul's description of how to fight the Enemy's attack. I especially love the imagery in verses 10–13:

Finally, be strong in the Lord and in the strength of His might. Put on the full armor of God, so that you will be able to stand firm against the schemes of the devil. For our struggle is not against flesh and blood, but against the rulers, against the powers, against the world forces of this darkness, against the spiritual forces of wickedness in the heavenly places. Therefore, take up the full armor of God, so that you will be able to resist in the evil day, and having done everything, to stand firm. (NASB)

Let's look at these verses more closely in light of our fight against Satan's lies about our unworthiness:

Know whose armor it is

It would be easy to skip right over those few words, but look at them: "Put on the full armor *of God*" (emphasis added). It is God's armor. Not armor made for you by God. But God's armor. Think about that for a second. You have complete and total access to the armor *of God*. It's as if God is saying, "Here, here is *my* armor. Put it on." I don't know a whole lot about armor, but I do know this from all my years reading adventure books from the library: the king always had the best, strongest, most expensive armor.

Know why you need it

I am not so much of a rule follower as some might imagine (shocking, I know). I have a hard time doing things just because someone tells me to, so understanding why I need to do it is always helpful for me. God tells us in this verse, "Put on the full armor of God, *so that you will be able to stand firm against the schemes of the devil*" (Ephesians 6:11 NASB, emphasis added).

I looked up "stand firm" in the original text and it literally means, "to take a battle-ready stance." This makes me think of fencers (read: swashbuckling swordsmen) and the way they stand when they are about to fight. Their "ready stance" allows them to be quick and flexible, able to withstand a blow and defend against multiple attacks. I've never held a real sword yet (but heaven knows, with a house full of boys, I've held my share of plastic swords), but I get this. Put on the full armor of God and stand ready. If I do so, I "will be able to *stand firm against the schemes of the devil*" (emphasis added).

And finally ...

Know who your enemy is

"For our struggle is not against flesh and blood, but against the rulers, against the powers, against the world forces of this darkness, against the spiritual forces of wickedness in the heavenly places" (Ephesians 6:11 NASB).

Our struggle is not against our boss who wants us to work overtime.

Our struggle is not against our two-year-old who just gave up her naps or our teenager who needs rides to multiple sports practices.

Our struggle is not against our husband who wants to talk about his day or our friends who call at the wrong time.

Our struggle is not against the people at church who want us to volunteer in the toddler nursery, or the room parents at school who want us to bake two dozen cookies overnight.

Our struggle is not against our busy calendar.

Our struggle is not against people who have hurt us, or past wounds that haven't healed, or even the consequences of poor choices we have made in our lives.

If we believe that "fixing" the people in our lives will help us break busy, we're forgetting the root of our busyness: the lies Satan wants us to believe. Go back and read who our Enemy is in verse 11. Understanding our Enemy is critical to daily fighting and winning the battle against unworthiness.

Battle Plans

So how do we, as Christ followers, fight this battle?

Rest

Know that you were created by God for God. You will know this by daily connecting with him in prayer, Scripture, and song. I keep a list of Scripture I go to anytime I am tempted to believe I am not enough, and I pray that Scripture aloud.

Ready yourself

Go back and read Ephesians 6:10–18 and remember each part of the armor of God and what it is for.

Relate

We know from everything we have learned that we are created to live in relationship with others. Shame thrives when we live our lives unconnected from others. We must find and immerse ourselves in life-changing Christian community.

Recall

Most of us think if people knew our stories (the nitty-gritty, down-and-dirty of the worst parts of us) that no one could really love us. Shame thrives in secrecy. But when we recall the truth of who we are in Christ and bravely share how we have been changed, we destroy the power of shame. This is what I'm doing with you in this book — simply telling my stories and how Jesus has changed my heart, my actions, and my life.

Remember

Whenever I feel a certain way about myself (afraid, unworthy, dumb, incapable), I ask God, in prayer, to help me remember the first time I felt that way. Sometimes, if the feeling or emotion is too strong, I ask a friend to pray with me. Pinpointing the exact first time I remember feeling that way — discovering its source — helps me to reject the lie and pull it out at its root.

Realize

We all fall into traps of feeling insecure and unworthy. For me, I get tempted to post too much on social media just to get the instant feedback from people instead of finding rest in Jesus. Realizing my actions are rooted in insecurity helps me catch myself before I post too much and go fishing for positive comments.

I spent a lifetime struggling to feel I had value in this world. Eventually, I discovered that no amount of striving, working to please others, or trying to prove myself was going to help me find my worth. All of that striving was just going to make me busy and miserable.

Your cycle of busyness may look different than mine. You

may be striving daily for that family member to finally tell you they love you and are proud of you, or to be the "right" kind of Christian in the eyes of others, or maybe even to discover what God has created you for on this earth. But none of those things determine your worth.

If we are going to break busy and find our worth in a world of striving, we need to put away our striving and rest in the beauty of this Scripture:

> But God, being rich in mercy, because of the great love with which he loved us, even when we were dead in our trespasses, made us alive together with Christ — by grace you have been saved — and raised us up with him and seated us with him in the heavenly places in Christ Jesus, so that in the coming ages he might show the immeasurable riches of his grace in kindness toward us in Christ Jesus. For by grace you have been saved through faith. *And this is not your own doing*; it is the gift of God, not a result of works, so that no one may boast. (Ephesians 2:4 – 9 ESV, emphasis added)

The best things in your life? They are not of your own doing. They are not because of who you are or what you accomplish, but because of who God is and what he has already accomplished.

God showed us how much we are worth by giving us everything: grace, salvation, and eternal life. Our greatest calling is to receive his gift.

Action Steps

1. Remember a time in your life when you felt a deep sense of shame. What lie were you believing?

2. Identify an area of your life where your busyness is an attempt to prove your worth. What would change if you approached life from a deep sense of God's grace and love for you, rather than a sense of shame or pride?

3. Pray and ask God what truths he wants you to know about his love for you, and ask that he make love for him the central desire of your heart.

EPILOGUE

As I finished writing *Breaking Busy* and now write this epilogue, I have just wrapped up one of the fullest months I've had in a long time. It was filled with two speaking engagements, my responsibilities as executive director of Propel Women, a quick business trip to London, going on a field trip with my second grader to the zoo (mercy!), and end-of-the-school-year festivities for all five boys. Lots to do, lots of needs, and lots of places where I had to say no to opportunities, requests, and extra plans.

I chose what I could and wanted to do, and I politely declined everything else that wasn't 100 percent necessary this month. Before, I would make myself crazy doing everything because I felt I *had to* or I *should*. I've stepped off that hamster wheel of crazy busy and refuse to get back on!

Don't think it was easy for me to say no. It wasn't. The good fight against unnecessary busyness is an ongoing battle. (Remember, it's how the Enemy distracts us from our purpose in life!) If writing this book for me, or reading this book for you, was enough to magically fend off the constant pull of endless busyness, life would be so much easier.

We never wake up one day and realize, "Whaddya know, life is a breeze. I don't have fifty things that need my full attention today or ten people who need me to help them. I guess I'll spend the day having a pedicure and letting someone peel grapes for me."

Every day is a battle to break busy and keep the tyranny of

the urgent from creeping in, a battle to hold precious our down time, a battle to keep our perspective and get quiet and connect with God.

As we close out our time together in this book, I want to be sure we never confuse a busy life with a full life. To me, a busy life is frazzled, harried, lived at a pace I'm not meant to live, doing things I'm not meant to do. A busy life is a life the Enemy has created in order to keep me from God's purpose. A full life, on the other hand, is a life lived in step with what God has called me to do. I like how Jesus said it in John 10:10: "The thief comes only to steal and kill and destroy; I have come that they may have life, and have it to the full."

● ● ● ● ● ●

BREAKING BUSY IS A WAY OF LIFE.

Life for me and for you is full. Jesus' life was full. We are meant to stretch and grow and let God bring us to a new capacity level we didn't know we had. Living a full, happy life means we get to say no to unnecessary crazy, we don't have to be all things to all people, and we don't have to fill our lives with things because we think we should.

Breaking Busy Together

Let's continue together! I would love for us to encourage and support each other in our breaking busy journey to live lives not for what other people expect, but for what Jesus calls us to do, to fight the lies of the Enemy with truth and continually renew our thoughts and focus on whose we are, not what we think we need to do.

#BreakingBusy

A fun way to encourage each other is to stay connected by using #BreakingBusy on Facebook, Instagram, and Twitter. Every time you catch yourself rejecting the Enemy's lies, the unnecessary expectations of others, and the unhealthy expectations you put on yourself — share it! The breaking busy lifestyle isn't about dictating how anyone "should" live, but about being generous to ourselves and others and encouraging each other to live as God has called us.

Breaking Busy Resources

You can find a downloadable decision-making framework, time assessment form, and lots more free gifts to help you live the life you were created to live. Go to AlliWorthington.com/BreakingBusy for more.

Breaking Busy Groups

If you are interested in starting your own Breaking Busy group to take the journey with your friends, you can download everything you need on the website for free. (Don't we all love free?)

Remember, you do not have to strive endlessly to be good enough or to find God's plan for you. When you stay focused on God, you will not miss your destiny. Listen for his nudging in your spirit and through his Word. Living in his will and through his power can never be done while living a life of frazzled crazy busyness.

My prayer is that *Breaking Busy* helps to remind you that you have permission to be the person God created you to be and permission to live the full, wonderful life he created you to live.

ACKNOWLEDGMENTS

There aren't enough words to properly thank everyone who helped this book become a reality. From my family, my friends, my editors, to the people in my life who lived out the stories with me — I am so thankful for you all.

My Savior

Thank you, Jesus, for your furious pursuit of me. Thank you for finding me when I try to run away and hide from you. Thank you for forgiving me when I don't deserve it. Thank you for empowering me to do what I could never do on my own. And thank you for constantly reminding me who I am and whose I am. Bind my wandering heart to thee.

My Family

Justin, Jack, Joey, James, and Jeremiah — You have my heart. I love each of you tremendously. It is my great honor to steward the responsibility of being your mom and helping you become all God has called you to be. Every day you make me proud, make me laugh, make me a little grossed out; and I wouldn't have it any other way. Thank you for putting up with months of Saturdays where I was locked in my bedroom writing this book.

Jessica — You have grown up to be a beautiful, brilliant, and vivacious woman. I am so proud of you. You are a gift!

Debbie — You are the best mother in the world. Thank you

for raising a little girl who always knew, even in the toughest of circumstances, she was loved by you and by Jesus. Thank you for giving me that.

Anna — Thank you for raising such a great man. I am forever in your debt.

Bob, Sue, John, Nancy, Pam, Sammi, Evonne, Robert, Megan, Seth, Zach, Shelby, Leanne, Brant, Will, Emily, Parker, Josh, Rob, James, Beth, Liam, Adele, Christina, Jacob, Gregg, Kristen, Lily, William — I love you all.

My Friends

Megan Jordan — I am so grateful for how you speak into my life with honesty, humor, and wisdom. I could never ask for a better friend. I love you.

Carol Jones — I never could have dreamed of a better mentor, friend, and partner in kingdom work. I am so grateful to you and all you have poured into my life. You are a great woman of God, and I'm lucky to call you my friend. Thank you for your trust.

Barbara Jones — Our BlissDom days are over, but our friendship never will be. Thank you for believing in me in those early days, for making me get up on that stage even though I was terrified, and for showing me the ropes of playing way above my comfort zone.

Tami Heim — Over the past three years, you have been part of the life-changing moments. Thank you for your wise counsel, patience, and unflinching support.

My Colleagues

Jenni Burke — Thank you for believing in me and for pushing me to learn to write like a grown-up, and for lovingly smacking down my worst ideas with grace.

Sandra Vander Zicht — Thank you for encouraging me to write at a level I never imagined I had in me. You helped take this book to a new level, and I am so grateful to you.

Lori Wilson — Thank you for designing such a beautiful cover for this book. Your energy, your vision, and your belief in this book mean so much to me.

My BlissDom Family

There's not a day that goes by that I don't learn from you, laugh with you, and marvel at the lives you live with strength, courage, and kindness. BlissDom was and will always be a story of what happens when the brightest, kindest people come together to celebrate each other's dreams. Thank you all for teaching me about the power of community and for being such an important part of this story:

Abby Barnhart, Abby Hollingsworth, Abby Lawson, Aimee Giese, Alece Ronzino, Alicia Ybarbo, Alison Kramer, Alison Olfelt, Allison Czarnecki, Allison MacDonald, Amanda Henson, Amber (and Seth!) Haines, Amber Maduell, Amber Marlow, Amy Allen Clark, Amy Halloran, Amy Locurto, Amy Smith, Amy Tucker, Amy Turn Sharp, Ana L. Flores, Anada Leeke, Angela England, Angie Arthur, Angie Lynch, Anisa Meyhew, Ann Imig, Anna Epp, Anna Laffer, Anne Parris, Annie Downs, Asha Dornfest, Ashleigh Baker, Ashley Ousley, Audrey McClelland, Becca Ludlum, Beki Hastings, Beth Anne Balance, Beth Fletcher, Bianca Juarez-Olthoff, Bree Hester, Brene Brown, Bridget Ivey, Carla Birnberg, Carmen Stacier, Caroline Edwards, Carrie Isaac,

Carrie Weir, Casey Mullins, Catherine Conners, C. C. Chapman, Cecily Kellogg, Charlene Oliver, Chris Ann Brekhus, Chris Mann, Christine Farnum, Christine Koh, Christine Satterfield, Christine Young, Claire Diaz-Ortiz, Claire Larson, Courtney Widmore, Dana Hilmer, Dana Loesch, Daniel C. White, Danielle Smith, Darlene Weir, David and Tammy Molnar, Dawn Camp, Deanna Garretson, Deb Rogers, Dedra Herod, Diana Stone, Dina Freeman, Donielle Baker, Elan Morgan, Ellen Seidman, Emily Elling, Emily P. Freeman, Erica Mueller, Erin Kennedy, Erin Loechner, Fadra Nally, Hannah Braboy, Heather Barmore, Heather King, Heather Sokol, Heather Solos, Heather Sprittibee, Heather Tenney, Holly Buchanan, Holly Hamaan, Holly Temple, Jamie Reeves, Jana Warnke, Janice Croze, Jeanette Kaplun, Jeff Goins, Jen Lancaster, Jen Murray, Jenn Fowler, Jenn Schmidt, Jennifer Doyle, Jenny Ingram, Jenny Martin, Jessica Erickson, Jessica Turner, Jessica Weaver, Jill Anderson, Jill Krause, Jim Lin, Jodi Grundig, Jody Halstead, Joey Fortman, John and Brooke Morgan, Jo-Lynne Shane, Jon and Jenny Acuff, Julie Cole, Justin McCollough, Kacia Hosmer, Karen Hammonds, Karen Walrond, Karin Taylor, Kasey Trenum, Kate Bryan, Katherine Stone, Katie Clemmons, Katie Kimball, Katie York, Kelby Carr, Kelley Phillips, Kelli Stuart, Kelly Hancock, Kelly Olexa, Kevin Carroll, Kim Borchet, Kristen Luna, Kristen Tierney, Kristen Welch, Kristi Bonnie, Kristin Potler, Kristy Bartlett, Kyran Pittman, Lara Valez, Laura Bleill, Laurie Turk, Leah Dusek, Leah Segedie, Leigh Grey, Leslie Dougherty, Linda Sellers, Lindsay Maines, Lindsey Cheney, Lisa Lehmann, Lisa Leonard, Lisa Nelson-Woods, Lisa-Jo Baker, Lora Fanning, Liz Strauss, Liza Hippler, Lotus Carroll, Lucrecer Braxton, Maggie Whitley, Malia Carden, Malise Terrell, Mandy Rose, Mariah Humphries, Mariah Leeson, Marie LeBaron, Mary Carver, MaryAnne Beasley, Maya Bisineer, Meagan Francis, Megan Tietz, Meghan Tucker, Melanie Feehan,

Acknowledgments

Melanie Nelson, Melinda Roberts, Melissa Duncan, Melissa Michaels, Melissa Stover, MeRa Koh, Meredith Pelham, Meredith Sinclair, Michael and Gail Hyatt, Michelle Lamar, Michelle McGraw, Michelle Sarabia, Mishelle Lane, Molly Thornburg, Molly Wey, Monica Barnett, Monique Frausto, Myquillyn Smith, Nancy Doud, Nancy Smith, Nate St. Pierre, Nichole Smith, Nicolas Romero, Nicole Shumacher, Nish Weiseth, Pam Case, Paula Bruno, Rachel Herrscher, Rachel Matos, Rachel Matthews, Rachel McPhillips, Renee Ross, Ria Sharon, Rita Arens, Robin Dance, Robin O'Bryant, Ruthanne Genco, Sami Cone, Sandy Coughlin, Sara Bane, Sara Hawkins, Sara Sophia, Sarabeth Jones, Sarah Hawkins, Sarah Kimmel, Sarah Pinnix, Sarah Turner, Sarah Visbeek, Scott Stratton, Selena Cochran, Shannon Litton, Shannon McKarney, Shannon Mischuk, Sheila Marcelo, Shell Rouse, Shelley Kramer, Sherrie Smith, Sili Recio, Simon Salt, Sommer Poquette, Stephanie Buckley, Stephanie McCratic, Stephanie Precourt, Stephanie Smirnov, Sue Duffield, Sugar Jones, Susan Cain, Susie Parker, Tammy Munson, Tania Sanders, Tanis Miller, Tara Robertson, Tiffany Manley, Tsh Oxenreider, Wendy Scherer, Yoly Mason.

With love always.
xoxo,
Alli

NOTES

1. Ray Williams, "Why 'Busyness' Is Not Productivity," *Psychology Today*, July 22, 2012. Accessed May 9, 2015.

2. American Psychological Association, "Stress in America: Mind/Body Health: For a Healthy Mind and Body, Talk to a Psychologist," 2010, http://www.apa.org/news/press/releases/stress/2010/key-findings.aspx.

3. Sarah Young, *Jesus Calling* (Nashville: Thomas Nelson, 2004), 179.

4. Tara Parker-Pope, "When Sex Leaves the Marriage," *New York Times*, June 3, 2009, http://well.blogs.nytimes.com/2009/06/03/when-sex-leaves-the-marriage/?_r=1.

5. Janet Kornblum, "Study: 25% of Americans Have No One to Confide In," *USA Today*, June 22, 2006.

6. Stephanie Coontz, "How to Stay Married," *London Times*, November 30, 2006.

7. Alex Greig, "All the Lonely Facebook Friends," *Daily Mail*, September 12, 2013, http://www.dailymail.co.uk/news/article–2419419/All-lonely-Facebook-friends-Study-shows-social-media-makes-MORE-lonely-unhappy-LESS-sociable.html.

8. Rick Warren, *The Purpose Driven Life*, exp. ed. (Grand Rapids, MI: Zondervan, 2012), 17.

9. Jennie Allen, *Anything* (Nashville: Thomas Nelson, 2012), 12.

10. *Merriam Webster's Collegiate Dictionary*, 11th ed., s.v. "edit."

11. Steven Furtick, *Sun Stand Still: What Happens When You Dare to Ask God for the Impossible* (Colorado Springs: Multnomah, 2010), 90.

12. Psalm 23:1–6 NASB.

13. Sonja Lyubomirsky, *The Myths of Happiness: What Should Make You Happy, but Doesn't, What Shouldn't Make You Happy, but Does* (New York: Penguin, 2014).

14. Tanya Lewis and LiveScience, "Emotions Can Be Contagious on Online Social Networks," *Scientific American Global* RSS, July 1, 2014. Accessed December 7, 2014.

15. Jeff Goins, "The Discipline of Gratitude [Slow Down Challenge: Day 5]." Goins Writer RSS. Accessed December 7, 2014, http://goinswriter.com/gratitude/.

16. Ibid.

17. Alli Worthington, "Why I Won't Be Getting You a Christmas Present," *Babble*, December 9, 2013, http://www.babble.com/babble-voices/why-i-wont-be-getting-you-a-christmas-present/. Accessed January 29, 2015.

18. For more information, see Alli Worthington, "How to Work Less and Do More," Alli Worthington blog, April 1, 2014, http://alliworthington.com/work-less-and-do-more/.

19. Term coined by Charles Hummel, *Tyranny of the Urgent* (Downers Grove, IL: InterVarsity, 1967, 1994).

20. Andy Stanley, *The Principle of the Path* (Carol Stream, IL: Tyndale House, 2008), 14.

21. Suzy Welch, *10–10–10: A Fast and Powerful Way to Get Unstuck in Love, at Work, and with Your Family* (New York: Scribner, 2010).

22. Chip Heath and Dan Heath, *Decisive: How to Make Better Choices in Life and Work* (New York: Crown Business, 2013).

23. Edward Mote (1797–1874), "My Hope Is Built," *United Methodist Hymnal*, http://www.hymnsite.com/lyrics/umh368.sht.